YOURSELF AUGMENTED

Tell your Manager "I'm Not Replaceable"

VINEETH ELLORE,
SANDEEP SHEKHAR

Clever Fox® PUBLISHING
Chennai • Bangalore

CLEVER FOX PUBLISHING
Chennai, India

Published by CLEVER FOX PUBLISHING 2025

ISBN: 978-93-7500-040-2

TABLE OF CONTENTS

CHAPTER 1

AUGMENTING YOURSELF

The word *"augmenting"* has been buzzing in sales circles lately. But what does it really mean? Where did it come from? And why is it suddenly such a critical idea in our profession?

To understand its importance, we first need to rewind back to the time before AI became part of our daily workflow.

Before the Age of AI

Sales used to be slow.

Not because we lacked ambition, but because we had to do everything manually. Researching prospects. Writing outreach. Performing admin tasks. Coaching one-on-one. It was all on us.

Yes, we had software—but those tools were "helpers," not "doers."

Take email outreach, for example. A sales tool might track open rates or responses, but you still had to:

- Research your prospect
- Join the dots
- Write the message
- Experiment with subject lines and formats

The grunt work was still yours.

After AI Arrived

Today, the game has changed. We're in an era where software doesn't just assist—it *acts*. AI can:

- Research prospects
- Generate messaging
- Join the dots instantly
- Run entire outreach cadences with no human intervention

And this brings us to the big question:

What does *augmenting yourself* mean in the context of sales?

Market Segments and AI's Role

Sales isn't one-size-fits-all. Whether you sell to SMBs, mid-market, enterprises, or strategic accounts, the approach changes.

AI's value also shifts across these segments. But in every segment, augmenting yourself means **becoming a superhuman compared to your pre-AI self.**

This leads to one of the most important debates in modern sales:

Human + AI or Human vs AI?

Three Possible Futures

We can imagine three broad scenarios:

1. Human-Only Sales

Picture an SDR sending 50 personalized messages and making 100 calls a day without AI. Even at the fastest pace, it could take 10–20 minutes to research and craft each message. That's 500 minutes—more than a full workday for just one task.

Without AI, you'd need templates and automation, which inevitably lead to generic, low-quality outreach.

2. AI-Only Sales

In theory, AI could identify the best prospects, research them, craft personalized messages, send them, follow up, and book meetings. This is the vision behind the "AI SDR."

In reality, it falls short. AI still struggles to capture *true* personalization, subtle context, or the human "show me you know me" effect. It can't create genuine moments of connection that make a prospect feel valued.

3. Human + AI Sales *(The Winner)*

Here's the sweet spot. AI handles 95% of the manual work research, writing drafts, scheduling, and data entry while you focus on the 5% that makes all the difference: building relationships, asking the right questions, and creating trust.

Why Humans Still Matter

An AI SDR might cost your company $500–$2,000 a month. Your salary is 5–10x that. To justify your value, you need to deliver something AI can't:

authentic human relationships.

AI will never:

- Shake a prospect's hand
- Share a lunch conversation
- Read a room in real time

Sales is still built on trust—trust in you and in your product. No one is going to sign a $100,000 deal with a chatbot alone.

Learning from History

When industrial machines arrived, factory workers feared for their jobs. But over time, people learned to work *with machines*, not against them.

AI in sales is the same. Think of it as the massive factory machine doing 95% of the work while you supervise the inputs and outputs, applying your judgment and experience.

The Power of Context

Even with a bigger "context window," AI will never match the decades of lived experience in your head. If you've spent 25–50 years learning how people buy, negotiate, and build trust, that knowledge can't simply be replicated.

This is why AI should be your thinking partner, not your replacement.

What a Fully Augmented Seller Looks Like

A *100% augmented* salesperson:

- Spends all most their time on relationship-building and revenue-generating activities
- Delegates all non-revenue, admin, and research tasks to AI
- Uses freed-up time to upskill and deepen market expertise

- Operates like AI were their personal chief-of-staff

In this model, AI enables you to become a true **superhuman in sales**—faster, sharper, and more focused than ever before.

This is the future of selling.

Not AI replacing you, but AI amplifying you. Not Human *versus* AI, but Human *plus* AI.

In the next chapter, we'll explore exactly how sales has evolved over the past two decades, and why this "New Age of Selling" demands that you not just keep up—but augment yourself to lead.

CHAPTER 2

THE NEW AGE OF SELLING

In the last chapter, we explored what it means to augment yourself with AI—why the future isn't Human vs. AI, but Human + AI.

But to appreciate just how transformational this moment is, let me rewind the clock back to when I first stepped into sales in 2005.

Because the truth is: selling today is nothing like selling in 2005. And tomorrow? It won't look like today.

2005–2010: The Age of Persistence (The "Tell Me" Economy)

In 2005, SaaS wasn't yet saturated. Salesforce was still convincing the world that "software in the cloud" was viable. The average VP of Sales wasn't being hammered by 200 cold emails a week. Buyers were curious—and cautious.

That's why **logos were the ultimate trust signal**. If you could say, *"We already work with IBM, Microsoft, and Oracle"*, doors opened. Buyers thought:

- *If IBM trusts you, I should at least listen.*
- *If Microsoft uses your product, you must be credible.*

It wasn't about case studies or ROI calculators—it was about association. Borrowed trust.

Here's what a real talk track looked like back then:

"Hi [Prospect], I'm with XYZ Software. We work with IBM, Microsoft, and Oracle to streamline compliance reporting. I'd love to schedule 30 minutes to show you how we could do the same for your team."

That was enough. Flashing a big customer logo built instant trust. Because in 2005, SaaS itself was still new. Competition was limited. Buyers didn't have 20 vendors to choose from.

It wasn't elegant, but it worked. Persistence and brand association got the job done.

2010–2015: The Age of Relevance

By the early 2010s, things started to shift. Buyers got more skeptical. They had more vendors knocking on their door, and they weren't handing out 30 minutes so easily anymore.

This was when **relevance became king.**

It wasn't enough to say "we work with IBM." You had to prove you understood *their* business. That meant digging for signals—funding announcements, expansion plans, leadership hires—and weaving those into your outreach.

A message from this era might sound like:

"Congrats on the $20M funding round and your new London office! Companies in expansion mode often struggle with GDPR compliance. We recently helped [Competitor] speed up their audits by 40%. Worth a quick chat?"

Notice the shift. Less "look at us." More "I see what's happening with you."

Relevance separated the average SDR from the good ones.

2015–2020: The Age of Personalization

By 2015, **relevance alone wasn't enough**. Every SDR had learned to "find a trigger" and "add context." Suddenly, inboxes were full of semi-relevant, templated emails:

- *"Congrats on the Series B!"*
- *"Saw you just hired a VP of Sales!"*

The problem? Everyone was doing it. Prospects got numb to it.

This ushered in what I call the **"Prove It" economy**.

You couldn't just say "I know you." You had to *show them you knew them*. That's where **social channels** like LinkedIn, Twitter, and industry forums became goldmines.

This was the **shift from surface-level personalization to meaningful relevance**. If the 2005–2010 era was about persistence, and 2010–2015 was about relevance, this era demanded that you *prove you knew the person*—not just the account.

A sales talk track here might sound like:

"Hi Sarah, I saw your LinkedIn post about how tough it's been onboarding remote sales teams post-acquisition. That reminded me of a conversation I had with another VP of Sales at a $200M ARR SaaS firm—they had a nearly identical challenge. Would you be open to hearing how they structured their playbook to fix it?"

See the difference? It's not *"I see you like golf."* That's trivia. Instead, it's connecting **the buyer's lived reality** to a **business solution**.

This wasn't generic personalization. It was **showcasing effort, care, and insight**, while still tying back to the prospect's burning problem.

This era was also when "logos + relevance" wasn't enough anymore. Buyers expected you to know them as humans, not just accounts.

2020–2025: The Rise of AI and Social Selling

Fast-forward to the 2020s, and sales has never been harder—or more exciting.

AI has exploded into our workflows. Prospect research that once took three hours now takes 30 seconds. Writing 10 tailored emails can be done in minutes. SDRs have access to more tools, data, and automation than ever before.

And yet… the game has gotten tougher.

Why? Because buyers' mental **filters are sharper**. Spam detection isn't just in inboxes—it's in people's heads. They can smell a mass-produced pitch a mile away.

This is why **pattern interrupts and precision personalization** are so critical. If you open with the same tired "Can I have 30 seconds to explain why I'm calling?" script, buyers will tune you out.

Instead, it's about connecting the dots faster and better than your competition.

For example:

"Hi [Prospect], I noticed your company just expanded into Europe with a new London office. I see that with the new $20M funding round, you're hiring 12 enterprise AEs. That usually means your new reps are about to be bombarded by legal on compliance. ISO and SOC are covered for US, but GDPR isn't yet listed on your site for your EU expansion. Are you already planning for that?"

That's modern selling: weaving together **AI-powered insights** with human intuition to make the outreach feel fresh, timely, and valuable.

And social selling? Still massively underutilized. A well-placed LinkedIn DM, grounded in what a prospect is actually posting about, can outperform 100 cold calls.

We'll dive deeper into how modern social selling works and how it can instantly catapult you to the top of the ladder in a later chapter.

The reps who win today don't just hustle harder. They hustle smarter with AI as their companion.

2025–2030: The Age of Psychology

So where does this all lead?

The next frontier isn't about *more tech.* It's about **understanding people at scale.**

AI will soon handle 95% of the heavy lifting: research, drafting, scheduling. But the 5% left—the part that makes or breaks deals—comes down to psychology.

How do people make decisions?

What fears drive their objections?

What motivates them to buy now versus later?

The reps who master psychology—who know how to adapt their talk track to a DISC profile, frame a story that resonates, or mirror a prospect's style—will be the ones who thrive.

Because as AI matures, the question will shift: *why is a human even in the loop?*

The answer can't just be "to send emails." AI can already do that.

The answer has to be: "to create trust, influence, and insight that no algorithm can replicate."

It's not that using 2015-style personalization won't work today. It still does.

But it won't make you the **top 1%**.

The bar is higher now. Buyers are sharper. AI is blurring the line between what's human and what's automated.

That's why you must **augment yourself.**

You need to truly understand your role in this new world. You need to tame AI and make it your companion.

If you don't, someone else will and they'll replace you.

This is the New Age of Selling: not just more activity, but smarter activity at scale. Not AI versus human, but human plus AI.

And that leads us directly to the next chapter: **What is Psychology in Sales?** Because in the age of AI, the biggest differentiator isn't just data. It's understanding people.

CHAPTER 3

WHAT IS PSYCHOLOGY IN SALES?

In the last chapter, we looked at how the *New Age of Selling* is shaped by AI, changing buyer expectations, and the need for human–AI augmentation.

But even in this AI-driven era, there's something that technology can't fully replicate: the human ability to understand, connect with, and influence another person.

That's where psychology enters the picture.

Sales Isn't Just a Process — It's a Human Decision Game

When people talk about sales, they often think about the mechanics:

- Send a cold email
- Engage inbound prospects
- Run discovery calls
- Deliver demos
- Handle pricing discussions

- Negotiate and close

If that's all there was to it, every rep would be hitting 100% of quota every quarter.

But they don't, because sales isn't just about running a process. It's about understanding *people.*

The best reps aren't just selling a product. They're guiding a human being toward a decision. That's where trust is built. That's where authentic relationships start. And that's where psychology in sales becomes the quiet differentiator.

The "Gut Feeling" You Already Use

If you've ever had a gut feeling about a deal, you've already used psychology — you just may not have called it that.

For example, you're on a discovery call. You've asked all the right questions, but the prospect stays guarded. You leave the call thinking, *This deal probably isn't going anywhere.*

That instinct came from picking up subtle cues — tone, pacing, body language, hesitation — and forming an internal judgment. Psychology gives you a way to turn those instincts into a structured, repeatable skill.

From Instinct to Structure

Since the 1940s, psychometric research has given us tools to understand human behavior in a predictable way. One of the most effective frameworks for sales is the **DISC assessment**.

DISC doesn't guess at someone's deep personality over their whole life — it focuses on **behavioral preferences** in a specific context. In sales, that's gold.

The Basics of DISC

DISC is built around four primary behavior styles:

1. **Dominance (D)** – Fast-paced, results-oriented, competitive. Motivated by winning, efficiency, and control.
2. **Influence (I)** – Outgoing, persuasive, enthusiastic. Motivated by relationships, recognition, and excitement.
3. **Steadiness (S)** – Patient, supportive, dependable. Motivated by stability, harmony, and trust.
4. **Conscientiousness (C)** – Precise, analytical, detail-focused. Motivated by accuracy, quality, and logic.

Unlike models like the Big Five (OCEAN) that define *who you are* across all life contexts, DISC focuses on *how you behave* in a given environment, which makes it much easier to apply directly in a sales conversation.

Why DISC Works in Sales

Every buyer processes information differently. If you present the exact same pitch to everyone in the same way, you're asking them to adapt to you and they won't.

Top reps flip that around: they adapt their communication to match the buyer's style.

Think back to when you were a kid. You probably learned early that you could ask your mother for something one way, and your father another way — because you knew how each would respond. Same information, different framing. That's DISC in action.

Example: Selling Payroll Software with DISC

Scenario:

"Our payroll software sometimes calculates overtime incorrectly, and we need to fix it before the next payroll cycle."

Dominance (D) – Direct, Results-Focused

"The overtime bug could cost us money and credibility. Let's choose the fastest fix so we can guarantee error-free payroll this cycle."

(Risk, urgency, quick win)

Influence (I) – Social, Enthusiastic

"Some employees noticed their overtime pay wasn't quite right — we don't want that to be the story going around! Let's team up and come up with a solution that makes payroll something people rave about."

(Reputation, collaboration, positivity)

Steadiness (S) – Supportive, Consistent

"A few overtime payments came out wrong, and I'm concerned it might hurt employee trust. If we put a stable fix in place now, we can keep everyone confident in the system."

(Trust, stability, reliability)

Conscientiousness (C) – Detail-Oriented, Accuracy-Focused

"Audit reports show a 2% error rate in overtime calculations. We should review the algorithm, run simulations, and ensure the fix passes all tests before the next payroll run."

(Data, precision, thoroughness)

Same problem — four framings. Each one tuned to resonate with a specific behavioral style.

The Payoff

When you adapt your communication style to match the buyer's behavioral preference, two things happen:

1. The buyer feels understood — which accelerates trust.
2. Your message lands with maximum clarity — which accelerates decisions.

In the next chapter, we'll look at **how to quickly identify a prospect's DISC type** so you can apply this in real time throughout your entire sales journey.

CHAPTER 4

PSYCHOLOGY IN ACTION

From Theory to Application

In the last chapter, we explored the foundations of psychology in sales and what it takes to shine in today's era of B2B selling. We also introduced DISC as one of the most practical and powerful psychometric tools.

Now comes the crucial part: **putting psychology into action.**

Many sellers believe that adopting psychology in sales is a whole new ball game, something too abstract or "not for them." But the reality is much simpler. You already know your product and your value proposition. *Psychology doesn't add more content; it gives you a new lens*: reframing your message in a way that resonates with the person in front of you.

And here's the best part: you don't need fancy AI tools like Crystal or LeadLabs to do this (though they help). You can often identify a prospect's personality type in real time — during a Zoom call, a phone conversation, or even in a quick one-on-one at an event — simply by observing how they speak and behave.

The Power of DISC in Action

The DISC model divides personality into four core styles:

- **Dominance (D)** – Direct, decisive, results-driven
- **Influence (I)** – Expressive, social, persuasive
- **Steadiness (S)** – Patient, supportive, harmony-seeking
- **Conscientiousness (C)** – Analytical, precise, detail-oriented

But here's a nuance that many people miss: **most individuals are not purely one style.** They often exhibit a *blend* of two adjacent traits. For example:

- **D/I:** Energetic, assertive, charismatic; focused on results and persuasion.
- **I/S:** Outgoing and warm, but also patient and relationship-oriented.
- **S/C:** Dependable, steady, and highly detail-conscious.
- **C/D:** Structured, data-driven, but also decisive when needed.

This matters in sales because you'll often need to balance your approach. A **D/I** might want speed *and* energy; an **S/C** might want trust *and* detailed documentation.

Each style has **telltale cues** you can spot in live interactions. By noticing speech patterns, tone, body language, and choice of words, you can make an informed guess about which style you're dealing with — and then adjust your approach accordingly.

Observable Cues for DISC Personality Types

DISC Type	Speech & Voice	Body Language & Expressions	Interaction Style	Video Call Adaptation
Dominance (D)	Loud, firm, fast-paced; frequent interruptions; decisive tone	Upright, expansive posture; strong/steady eye contact; fewer smiles but intense expressions	Direct, task-focused, impatient with details, "cut-to-the-chase" style	Speaks most; drives agenda; interrupts to keep focus; confident tone noticeable even with limited visuals
Influence (I)	Lively, animated, varied pitch; fast, fluent, enthusiastic	Frequent smiles; animated facial expressions; wide gestures; leans forward	Storytelling, optimistic, persuasive, avoids conflict	Uses emojis/chat; over nods and reactions; expressive tone carries well over audio
Steadiness (S)	Soft, calm, slower pace; waits turn; minimal interruptions	Gentle smiles, frequent nods; relaxed, modest posture; avoids confrontational gaze	Supportive, agreeable, indirect or high-context style	Patient listener; may use "raise hand" instead of interrupting; polite feedback via nods/reactions
Conscientiousness (C)	Measured, precise, factual; careful word choice; moderate volume	Upright, still posture; steady gaze; restrained facial expressions; neat appearance	Analytical, structured, detail-focused; low-context, explicit communication	Well-organized (notes/screenshares); tidy background; clear, structured points even in virtual setting

This table can be used as a "cheat sheet" while you are on calls. But recognition is only half the job. The real impact comes when you apply DISC *stage by stage* in the sales process.

Step 2: Applying DISC Across the Sales Cycle

The sales cycle isn't a single conversation; it's a series of moments — discovery, demo, pricing, negotiation, and follow-up. Each DISC style requires a distinct psychological approach in every stage. The **Do's and Don'ts framework** from the research-backed playbook makes this practical.

Discovery Phase

- **D Style**: Be direct, cut the fluff, and show business impact quickly. Don't waste time on small talk or over-explain technical details.
- **I Style**: Engage in small talk, share stories, and emphasize innovation. Avoid overly technical deep dives or killing enthusiasm with too much caution.
- **S Style**: Slow down, listen patiently, and build personal trust. Avoid being aggressive or rushing decisions.
- **C Style**: Arrive with an agenda, data, and logical structure. Avoid vagueness or unsupported claims.

Product Demo Phase

- **D Style**: Keep it high-level, focused on results, and let them lead with questions. Don't drown them in technicalities.
- **I Style**: Make it interactive, high-energy, and fun. Avoid monotone, overly technical walkthroughs.
- **S Style**: Move step by step, link to reliability and practical ease of use. Don't rush or skip key explanations.
- **C Style**: Walk through logically, with detailed technical clarity and data. Don't gloss over steps or improvise.

Pricing Phase

- **D Style**: Frame pricing around ROI and value. Be direct, don't hesitate. Create urgency.
- **I Style**: Emphasize excitement and lifestyle improvements. Avoid nickel-and-diming or being overly formal.
- **S Style**: Highlight long-term stability, guarantees, and reduced risk. Avoid high-pressure tactics.
- **C Style**: Provide detailed breakdowns with logical justifications. Avoid vagueness or hidden costs.

Negotiation Phase

- **D Style**: Expect a tough stance; stay firm with data. Don't concede too quickly.

- **I Style**: Keep it collaborative and positive. Don't let things turn adversarial.
- **S Style**: Seek win-win, reassure them, and stay calm. Don't pressure them or overpromise.
- **C Style**: Stick to facts and logic; document everything. Don't agree to vague or unreasonable terms.

Follow-Up Phase

- **D Style**: Be concise, persistent, and ROI-focused. Don't rely on long casual emails.
- **I Style**: Check in personally, celebrate milestones, and keep energy alive. Don't only follow up when you need something.
- **S Style**: Provide structured onboarding and check-ins. Don't disappear or be inconsistent.
- **C Style**: Give regular reports, data updates, and track metrics. Don't be sloppy or treat it as a formality.

Real-World Discovery Call Examples

Theory is one thing, but let's look at how this plays out in practice. Below are **four roleplay examples** selling payroll software — where you start neutral, listen for 2–3 exchanges, and then adapt!

Example 1: Talking to a D

(Let's abbreviate the word Sales Person to "SP" here.)

Neutral Start

SP: "Thanks for making the time today. I'd like to understand your current payroll setup, what's working well, and where challenges are. Then I can share where we might help. Does that sound good?"

Prospect:

"Sure, but let's keep this quick. I've got another call soon."

SP (thinking): Time-sensitive, impatient. Possible **D**.

SP continues:

"Got it. What's the single biggest payroll headache your team faces right now?"

Prospect:

"Delays. If payroll slips even a day, I hear about it."

SP (thinking): Results-focused, intolerant of inefficiency → confirms **D**.

Adapted Response:

"Our clients typically cut payroll cycles by 70%. If we could guarantee same-day processing, is that the result you'd want to see?"

Example 2: Talking to a C

Neutral Start

SP: "Thanks for joining. My goal is to learn about your payroll process — what's working, what's not — and share how others are approaching it. Sounds good?"

Prospect:

"Yes. I'd like to know how your system handles compliance and reporting."

SP (thinking): Asks about compliance right away. Possible **C**.

SP continues:

"Great. Can you walk me through how you're handling payroll reconciliation today?"

Prospect:

"We reconcile monthly, but error tracking is manual. We lack a proper audit trail."

SP (thinking): Detail-heavy, accuracy-focused → confirms **C**.

Adapted Response:

"Our platform automatically generates audit logs every cycle, exportable in CSV or PDF, aligned with GAAP standards. Want me to share a sample compliance report?"

Example 3: Talking to an I

Neutral Start

SP: "Thanks for making the time. I'd love to learn about your payroll process — what's working, what's not — and then we can explore options. Does that work?"

Prospect:

"Absolutely! Oh, before we dive in — we just finished employee wellness week. It was amazing, but payroll made it tough to run stipends."

SP (thinking): Energetic, social, story-driven. Possible **I.**

SP continues:

"That sounds like a great program. How did payroll complicate it?"

Prospect:

"We had to fight the system to issue stipends. Honestly, I just want payroll to make employees happy, not stressed."

SP (thinking): People and experience focus → confirms **I**.

Adapted Response:

"That makes sense. Our system is built for flexibility — one-click stipends, fast processing, and employee-friendly reporting. Teams using us actually turn payroll into a positive employee moment."

Example 4: Talking to an S

Neutral Start

SP: "Thanks for joining today. I'd like to understand your payroll setup, what's working, and where things get tricky. Then we'll see if there's a fit. Okay?"

Prospect:

"That's fine. We've used the same system for years. It works, but lately the team feels stressed."

SP (thinking): Cautious, team-oriented. Possible **S**.

SP continues:

"Got it. Can you tell me more about what's been stressful?"

Prospect:

"The system is rigid. Our team puts in extra hours, and it's hurting morale. I want something smoother, but I don't want to push them too hard."

SP (thinking): Concern for harmony and stability → confirms **S**.

Adapted Response:

"Thank you for sharing that. Our clients often find their HR staff regain hours each week, making the process smoother and less taxing. we'll ensure the roll out is gradual and well-supported so your team feels cared for, not burdened."

Step 5: Psychology as a Sales Habit

This is what augmentation would look like. When applied consistently, DISC transforms selling. Instead of pushing one scripted pitch, you become adaptable — adjusting pace, tone, and emphasis depending on your buyer.

Most importantly, you realize that **buyers are often blended**. Recognizing that someone is **D/I** (results + energy) or **S/C**(trust + detail) helps you avoid oversimplification and makes your approach far more precise.

Psychology in sales is not manipulation. It is empathy in action. The best salespeople in the new age won't just sell products — they'll make buyers feel understood, respected, and confident in their decision. DISC, when practiced in real conversations, is one of the simplest and most effective ways to achieve that.

As we wrap up the psychology of selling, it's worth remembering that everything we do in sales, from the words we choose, to the tone we set, is built on how humans think, feel, and respond. But understanding psychology is only half the equation. The other half is knowing *where* those human behaviors now play out. And today in the B2B world, much of that happens online — in LinkedIn posts, comment threads, community spaces, and digital conversations that shape perceptions long before an email ever lands.

The next chapter explores how social selling has evolved from a buzzword into a real, measurable advantage for modern sellers. You'll see how to use the same psychological principles we just covered but apply them in the public arena where relationships are built before outreach ever happens. If psychology teaches you *why* people buy, social selling teaches you *where and when* they start trusting you.

CHAPTER 5

SOCIAL SELLING LIKE NOBODY DOES

In the last chapter, we discussed *psychology in sales* — how understanding the human behind the prospect changes the entire way you communicate. Social selling is where that psychology meets the digital arena. Here, the "stage" isn't a conference room or a phone call; it's LinkedIn, Twitter, or whatever platform your prospects live on. And just like with DISC, your edge comes from reading people, not just pushing a product.

What Social Selling Really Is (And Isn't)

I asked 500 salespeople what "social selling" means, most said: *"Oh, that's just commenting on people's posts."*

That's not wrong, but it's like saying *"running"* is the same as *"the Olympics."* Commenting is one *small* part of a much bigger, strategic approach.

At its core, social selling means **building relationships and social rapport** with your prospects before the pitch. It's not about selling *on* social media — it's about selling *through* the trust you create there.

Why Social Rapport Changes the Game

Let's compare two outreach cadences:

Scenario 1:

You send an email, a LinkedIn message, and make a cold call. The prospect has never heard of you. You're just another name in their inbox.

Scenario 2:

Before doing any of that, you've been liking their posts, leaving thoughtful comments, and maybe even sharing one of their articles with genuine appreciation. By the time your first email or call lands, your name feels familiar. Your connection rate jumps.

Which one do you think works better?

Exactly. And yet, fewer than **1% of reps** consistently put in this effort.

Why This Matters More Than Ever

With AI SDR tools and advanced automation (think Clay, Apollo, Lavender), *personalization at scale* has become incredibly convincing. But AI still struggles with

emotional signals — the subtle human touches that make a connection feel *real.* That's your advantage.

The mission: **show your prospect you're human before they even reply.**

Step 1: Craft an Authentic Connection Request

A blank connection request? Automation can do that.

A human connection request? That's about picking **signals only you can spot** — maybe a cause they support, a recent post, or a subtle detail from their profile.

If there's no personal signal, use the most recent company news or update. Recency signals stand out because they show you're paying attention *right now.* End your request with a **thoughtful, illuminating question**, not a generic "worth connecting?"

Step 2: Use Voice Notes & Video to Stand Out (Without Overthinking It)

Most SDRs freeze when they hear "send a voice note" or "record a quick video" — as if it's some elite, extrovert-only skill.

The reality? If you can write an email, you can send a voice note or video.

Think of it like this:

A voice note is nothing more than an email… read out loud in a friendly tone.

A video is that same email… but with your face and energy added in.

The trick is not to overcomplicate it. You already have the content — your cold email, follow-up, or value prop. The only difference is the format.

Here's how to make it effortless:

1. **Start with your existing email** — no reinventing the wheel.
2. Copy it into ChatGPT or Claude and ask:
   "Turn this into a casual 30-second voice note script for LinkedIn."
3. Practice it once — not ten times. Imperfection makes it feel human.
4. Hit record directly in LinkedIn (no fancy tools needed).

Pro tip: Keep it to **30–45 seconds**. Mention one specific, recent detail about them or their company to instantly prove it's not automated.

Example:

"Hey Alex, saw your recent post about expanding the customer success team — sounds like a big quarter ahead. That's exactly when payroll accuracy gets stress-tested…"

And here's the kicker: once you do this three or four times, it stops feeling like "public speaking" and starts feeling like talking to a coworker in Slack. The reps who embrace this are almost always the ones who cut through the noise — because automation can't fake tone, pacing, and real human warmth.

Step 3: Personalize Beyond AI — Leverage Personality Insights

If you've read the psychology chapter, you already know DISC and personality frameworks. In social selling, this means:

- Framing posts or DMs in a **results-driven tone** for high-D types.
- Using **enthusiasm and story** for I-types.
- Highlighting **trust and security** for S-types.
- Presenting **logic and proof** for C-types.

Yes, tools like Crystal Knows or LeadLabs can help. But manual observation — tone, post style, engagement habits — still wins.

Step 4: Build a Visible, Authentic Brand

This is the long game. Post insights, share stories, and engage in ways that show your expertise *and* personality.

When prospects search your name, they should see more than a job title.

Extras that work:

- Personal GIFs in DMs or follow-ups (not in first-touch emails — protect deliverability).
- Using humor and authenticity when it fits your style.
- Sharing small wins, lessons, and relevant industry content.

Note: The examples shown below in the table are not real comments, connection requests, or voice notes. These examples show how the same content can be portrayed differently.

DISC Type	Tone & Focus	Example Comment	Example Connection Request	Example Voice Note / Video Hook
Dominance (D) Direct, results-driven	Be concise, highlight wins, urgency, and competitive advantage.	"Your recent post on shortening sales cycles was 🔥. Cutting process time = revenue speed."	"Saw your post on sales ops efficiency. I've helped teams cut cycle time by 23%. Worth swapping notes?"	"Hey [Name], spotted you're leading a big market expansion — have an idea that could help hit those Q targets faster."
Influence (I) Social, story-driven	Use enthusiasm, stories, and community-building language.	"Loved your post about your SDR's win! Reminds me of when our team landed 3 deals in one week through LinkedIn."	"Really enjoyed your story about breaking into enterprise accounts. Would love to swap stories over coffee — virtually or IRL!"	"Your post about your first big deal made me smile. I've got a similar 'from cold to gold' story you'd enjoy."

Steadiness (S) Supportive, trust-oriented	Show empathy, reliability, and focus on stability.	"Your post on customer retention really resonated. trust is the core of every long-term deal."	"Appreciated your insights on building consistent client relationships. I've been working on similar approaches."	"Hi [Name], your comments on long-term partnerships hit home — I've got a framework for keeping 95% retention."
Conscientiousness (C) Detail & accuracy-focused	Be precise, reference data or proven processes.	"Your breakdown of sales funnel metrics was spot on. Especially the 18% drop at stage 2 is worth optimizing."	"Noticed your post on CRM automation. I have a 5-step workflow that's increased data accuracy by 12%."	"Hi [Name], Your post talked about precise execution. I can share a tested process that's eliminated data errors by 87% in payroll runs."

Bringing the Social Selling Loop Together

Social selling isn't a one-off tactic — it's a compounding edge.

It's the art of building familiarity, trust, and relevance *before* your first real conversation even starts.

Here's the loop in action:

1. **Warm up the connection** — like and comment thoughtfully on their posts.
2. **Send an authentic connection request** — anchored in a human-only signal.
3. **Stand out with a voice note or video** — keep it short, specific, and personal.
4. **Adapt to their personality type** — frame your value prop in their language.

Once you do this consistently, something powerful happens: prospects stop treating you like "just another SDR" in the queue. They *already* know your name, they already know you've been paying attention, and they're more likely to engage — not because you asked, but because you've earned it.

And here's the key — you don't need to roll out every element on Day 1. Start with one habit, practice it daily until it's second nature, then layer on the next.

Within weeks, you'll have a rhythm that feels natural and doesn't eat your day.

This is how you **prove you're human in a world of automation** — and why you'll always have an advantage over any AI-driven cadence. When done right, social selling isn't just an add-on to your outreach. It *is* the bridge that makes every future email, call, and meeting more likely to land.

Social selling taught us how to earn attention before we ever ask for it — how to build presence, share ideas, and start meaningful conversations in public spaces like LinkedIn and modern communities. But no matter how strong your social rapport becomes, relationships eventually need to move from digital to direct. Every connection request, every comment, every DM you send is really just setting the stage for one thing: a real conversation with a familiar face.

That's where cold calling comes in.

Cold calls remain one of the most decisive points of contact in B2B sales. They test not just your research or tone but your ability to think and adapt in real time. In the next chapter, we'll move from written words to spoken ones — from asynchronous to live interaction — and look at what makes a great cold call in the modern era of sales. Because while social selling helps prospects know you, a good cold call helps them *feel* that you understand them.

CHAPTER 6

COLD CALL 101

Cold calling isn't dead. It's misunderstood.

The reality? The phone is still the fastest way to generate pipeline—if you know how to use it.

The truth is that cold calling is 80% mindset and psychology, 20% talk track. You can have the perfect script in front of you, but if your mindset is off, the prospect hears it in your tone, your pauses, your energy. That's why this chapter starts not with the words, but with the **mental model of greatness.**

The Psychology of Great Cold Callers

Most people think the best callers are "naturals"—born extroverts who thrive on rejection. That's a myth.

Great callers aren't fearless. They're **prepared.** They understand sales is a skill, one that's practiced, refined, and sharpened like any other.

Here's the reality: if you're winging it on every cold call, you're gambling your quota. Top reps know you don't rise to the occasion—you fall to the level of your preparation.

Think of it like sports. Michael Jordan didn't just show up on game day and improvise. He practiced his fundamentals thousands of times so that in the heat of the game, his moves felt effortless. Cold calling is the same.

The Mindset: Selling Is Helping

When you call a stranger, you're not interrupting their day—you're potentially changing it.

This shift matters. Most SDRs and AEs sound nervous because they approach calls with a "take" mindset ("I need a meeting"). The greats flip it: they approach with a "give" mindset ("I might have something that helps you").

Your mantra before every call should be:

"I'm not here to sell. I'm here to help."

Because buyers don't buy from robots. They buy from humans who care about solving their problems.

The Greatness Checklist

Here's how the best consistently show up:

- ☐ **Pipeline Over Everything (POE)** – Always assume you don't have enough pipeline. Complacency kills momentum.
- ☐ **Plan the Attack, Attack the Plan** – Don't just dial. Go in knowing why this prospect matters.
- ☐ **Reach Out with Intention** – A call is not just "another activity." It's your shot at building trust.
- ☐ **Pre-Call Mantra** – Remind yourself: "I'm here to help."
- ☐ **Practice on Purpose** – Don't wait for live calls to train. Roleplay at least 3 times a week.
- ☐ **Metric Review** – Know your numbers: connect rates, conversion rates, and where you lose people.
- ☐ **Call Listening** – Review 3 calls weekly (your own or a teammate's). Spot patterns.
- ☐ **Decompress** – Cold calling is high-intensity. Build habits that release stress.
- ☐ **Seek Feedback** – Mentors, peers, and managers can spot what you miss.
- ☐ **Read & Learn** – At least one book a month. New perspectives expand your talk tracks.

This isn't a motivational poster. It's the bare minimum required to thrive in a world where buyers are bombarded daily.

Why Talking to Strangers Feels Hard

Here's the science: when you meet someone new, your brain is wired to size them up instantly. Fight-or-flight kicks in. Your prospect feels it too—they're subconsciously deciding if you're worth listening to before you've finished "Hello, this is…"

That's why **tone, pacing, and confidence** matter as much as your words.

The first 10 seconds set the stage for the entire call. If you sound apologetic, rushed, or robotic, you've lost before you started.

Remember: companies don't buy software. **People do.** Every prospect has stories, pressures, and fears that you can't see. Your job is to get past the title and connect with the human.

The Missing Ingredient: Emotion

One of the hardest parts of cold calling isn't handling objections or remembering the script—it's bringing real emotion into your voice.

Many reps have solid openers and can think on their feet, but they sound flat. Robotic. That kills even the best talk track.

The trick? **Visualize the prospect in front of you.** Imagine you're talking face-to-face on Zoom or Google Meet. Nobody has ever told you in real life, "You sound like a robot." Why? Because your brain naturally generates emotion when you see someone's expressions, posture, and energy.

Since you don't get those visual cues on a cold call, you have to simulate them. Pretend you're looking them in the eye. This flips a switch in your delivery—you sound natural, human, and trustworthy.

Cold calling isn't just about the words you say. It's about how those words feel coming out of your mouth.

The Cold Call Framework

Cold calls don't succeed because you memorize scripts. They succeed because you follow a framework that balances structure with authenticity.

Step 1: Open Strong

- Call with a clear purpose.
- Use insights that show you've done research (recent funding, hiring trends, competitive moves).

Example:

"Bob, from the research I saw, it looks like you're focused on hitting $50M ARR this year after raising $11M, and expanding your sales team into enterprise. Did I get that right, or am I missing something?"

Step 2: Anchor in Reality

Start by validating what they're doing right.

"That's awesome—you're investing in ABM and hiring aggressively. Many leaders we speak to are doing the same. But one challenge they keep running into is reps struggling to actually connect with prospects. Curious, is that something you're seeing as well?"

Step 3: Narrow the Problem

Gently guide them to surface-level pain and connect it to business outcomes.

"Interestingly, one culprit we've found is timing. If reps don't know when to call or what message resonates, pipeline goals start slipping fast. How does that compare to your world?"

Step 4: Sell the Meeting, Not the Discovery

Remember: the cold call's goal is not discovery, but a meeting.

"Do you have your calendar in front of you?" with "Does 2 pm tomorrow or 11 am the day after sound good?"

Step 5: Avoid the No-Show

Make sure you end the call by doing this…

"Last question before I let you get back to your day. Can you think of anything that might cause you to cancel or reschedule our meeting? And, if that happens, how'd you like to communicate back to me?"

The key: keep it light, professional, and helpful. Great cold calls feel like conversations, not ambushes.

Prepping with Dialers: Power vs Parallel

Not all cold calls start the same. Your dialer setup affects both your rhythm and your mindset.

Power Dialer: The Prep-Friendly Approach

A power dialer calls one prospect at a time, usually giving you **10–15 seconds** to prepare before someone picks up. That buffer is gold—it allows you to review notes, recall context, and open with confidence.

This makes power dialers perfect for more researched or contextual calls. You know who's picking up, which reduces fumbling and keeps conversations smoother.

⚡ Pro tip: Use AI to generate quick talk tracks while the line rings, or before your session begins. It keeps your openers sharp and contextual.

Parallel Dialer: The Volume Machine

Parallel dialers call **5–10 prospects at once**, which boosts activity metrics but can crush call quality. The challenge is that you don't know who will pick up. That's when mistakes happen—like mispronouncing a prospect's name. Instant credibility killer.

The fix:

- Take 1–2 seconds before speaking.
- Start without using their name until you've confirmed it. Example:

"Hi, this is Vineeth from Lead Labs. I know I'm calling you unannounced, but can I get 30 seconds to ask a relevant question?"

This buys you time to check their details before diving deeper.

Also, with parallel dialing, your opener must **roll off your tongue naturally.** You don't have time to test variants—so practice one strong opener until it's muscle memory.

Leveraging Voicemails

For years, sales teams have written off voicemails as a dead touchpoint. The reasons are consistent:

- **Prospects don't listen to them** (or so the story goes).
- **They take too long to leave** when you're focused on hitting activity numbers.
- **They're generic** — "Hey, just calling to see if you have 15 minutes..."
- **They carry an unrealistic ask** — usually a direct request for a callback.

And let's be honest: why should a prospect call you back? In most cases, they don't know you, don't trust you, and haven't been given any reason to spend their time. That's why voicemail response rates have plummeted and many teams have pulled them out of cadences entirely.

But here's the flip side: **because so few reps use voicemails well, the bar is incredibly low.** A well-crafted, contextual voicemail is now a differentiator. Instead of being "wasted effort," it becomes another touchpoint that strengthens your multi-channel presence and makes your outreach feel human.

The key is **context + small ask.**

Example Voicemail

"Hey John, looks like you were busy when I called. I saw your CEO Mike recently spoke about expanding to EMEA on his recent podcast with David. We've helped companies get GDPR compliant in less than two days. I've just hit send on an email and LinkedIn message as well-take a look when you get a chance, no need to call me back."

Notice what works here:

- Context (recent event, relevant to them).
- Credibility (how you've helped others).
- Small ask (just check email/LinkedIn, not "call me back").

Why Voicemails Work (When Done Right)

- Most reps don't use them—this makes you stand out.
- They create an extra touchpoint outside of email/social.
- They build rapport when tied to something specific.

A voicemail is your first chance to create a **human connection outside of social channels.**

How to Scale Voicemail Personalization

- **Manual method:** Export your prospect list, feed it into a foundational model (ChatGPT, Claude, Perplexity), ask it to surface timely insights about the company/prospect, then stitch that to your value prop. Downside: 30–40 minutes a day.

- **Automated method:** Use tools like LeadLabs to generate contextual talk tracks in one click. Faster, less manual friction.

⚠ Rule of thumb: never leave a voicemail just to "tick the box." Use it only when you can add real context and connection.

Why Most Reps Fail

Most reps either:

- Ramble with product pitches, or
- Freeze when they hear resistance.

The best know that cold calling isn't about closing. It's about **earning the right to continue the conversation.**

Every objection—"no budget," "send me an email," "we're happy with our vendor"—isn't a dead end. It's data. And if you handle it with composure, you turn "No" into "Not yet… let's talk."

That's why objection handling is its own chapter (and why it deserves the practice of an athlete, not the improvisation of an amateur).

Cold calling, at its core, is about creating conversations from nothing by turning a few seconds of uncertainty into a genuine dialogue. But once the call begins, the real skill isn't in just starting the conversation, it's in *sustaining* it. Because every prospect, no matter how warm or cold, eventually raises a question, a concern, or a flat-out objection.

That's where the next stage of selling begins.

The next chapter dives into one of the most misunderstood yet essential parts of sales — objection handling. You'll see how most objections aren't a rejection, but reflections of risk, timing, or misunderstanding. We'll unpack real scenarios, explore how top performers navigate them, and learn how to turn resistance into momentum.

CHAPTER 7

OBJECTION HANDLING: TURNING "NO" INTO "NEXT STEP"

Objections are not roadblocks—they're signals. They're your prospect telling you: *"I don't see the path yet. Show me."*

But here's the problem: most reps were never trained to handle "these signals" or objections (hate this word personally but let's use it anyway) in a structured way. They default to "winging it." That's why this chapter is designed to help you turn objections into **meetings, momentum, and ultimately revenue.**

The Psychology Behind Objections

Objections Are Not Personal

The biggest mistake new SDRs and AEs make is thinking an objection is a rejection of *them*. It isn't. Objections are friction points in the buyer's mind. They're filters—sometimes protective, sometimes defensive, often just reflexive.

Think about it: if you had dozens of reps reaching out to you daily, your brain would build shortcuts to say *"No, not now"* before even processing the request. That's not rejection—it's survival.

Objections Are Buying Signals

Counterintuitive, but true. Prospects who give you an objection are still engaged. They haven't ghosted. They haven't hung up. They're giving you data about how they think and what they fear. Top reps listen to objections as *clues* to the buyer's psychology.

For Example:

- *"We don't have budget right now."* → Translation: "I don't yet see enough value to justify moving money."
- *"Send me an email."* → Translation: "I don't trust you yet, and I want space to evaluate without pressure."
- *"We already have a vendor."* → Translation: "I don't see why switching is worth the effort."

Each of these is a chance to ask better questions, not push harder.

The Four Root Causes of Objections

Most objections are symptoms. Underneath them are usually one of these:

1. **Lack of Awareness** – They don't see the problem yet.
2. **Lack of Urgency** – They see the problem but it's not painful enough.
3. **Lack of Trust** – They don't trust you, your company, or the promise of your solution.
4. **Lack of Fit** – Rare, but sometimes they genuinely don't qualify even after building the list carefully.

If you don't diagnose which bucket an objection falls into, you'll respond incorrectly and lose momentum.

Handling Objections 101

This is the simplest framework you can use to handle any kind of objection.

Step 1: Pause & Listen

Never jump in defensively. Let the prospect fully articulate their thoughts. Sometimes, just letting them vent lowers resistance.

Step 2: Acknowledge & Validate

Psychologically, before you challenge someone, you need to agree with part of their reality.

Example:

- Prospect: *"We don't have a budget."*
- You: *"Totally fair. Budgets are tight everywhere right now."*

This lowers the wall.

Step 3: Reframe with Insight

Shift the perspective by anchoring to their bigger objective.

Example:

- *"That's exactly why our customers start small. Because even a 10% lift in pipeline coverage often pays for itself within the first quarter."*

Step 4: Ask Permission to Continue

Close the loop with a soft call-to-action.

- *"Would it make sense to set aside 15 minutes to explore whether this could actually help you hit your targets faster?"*

It might sound obvious or easy but the reality is that it can be hard to implement on live calls!

Turning Objections Into Meetings

Here's where most reps fail—they try to solve the entire objection *on the cold call.* The goal is not to win the argument. The goal is to win the meeting.

Let's take an example:

Prospect: *"We're happy with our current vendor."*

You: *"That's awesome. Most of our best customers felt the same at first."*

You (Reframe): *"Curious—what's the one thing you'd improve about your current setup if you could?"*

Prospect: *"Well, reporting is always a pain."*

You: *"That's exactly where we've been able to help companies like [Competitor Logo]. Would it make sense to spend 20 minutes comparing notes?"*

Notice, You didn't dismantle their current vendor. You redirected the conversation to a specific gap.

The Speed of Thought: Navigating the Three Buckets of Response

One of the hardest skills to master in cold calling is cognitive speed. You have milliseconds to process what the prospect just said and decide where to steer the conversation.

You don't lose conversations because you didn't have the perfect reply.
You lose them because you misread what the prospect actually said.

Most reps freeze on calls, not because they lack scripts or skills, but because the human brain cannot process how to handle 20 possible replies in real time. So instead of memorizing responses, you need something better:

A fast way to classify what kind of resistance you're facing, so you know exactly how to move the conversation forward.

When you ask a great open-ended question (let's say while selling LeadLabs) — like,

"How are you currently prioritizing which accounts to go after every single week from the several hundreds or thousands currently in your CRM?"

You might get twenty different variations of an answer. But after thousands of live calls, almost every response a prospect gives falls into **one of three buckets**:

1. **Vendor Centric** («We already use ZoomInfo.")
2. **Process Centric** («We score accounts internally on Salesforce.»)

3. **Ideology Centric** («We don't believe in prioritization; we just call everyone.»)

If you can instantly classify their answer into one of these three buckets, you don't need to panic. You just need to run the play for that bucket.

But if you can't, buy some time first! The simplest way to keep the conversation alive while your brain processes the "Bucket" is **Mirroring**.

Don't rush to pitch. If they say, *"We use ZoomInfo,"* you simply mirror: *"Oh, ZoomInfo?"*

If it's a positive response, validate them immediately: *"I'm glad you're using a solution for this already. Most people I talk to haven't even thought about it yet, so you're already steps ahead."*

If it's a negative response, *"It's not a priority right now"*. You mirror again, *"I've been hearing that lately from a few leaders, so you're not alone here."*

This buys you the mental bandwidth to classify their answer and execute the next move.

Let's take a look at each of the response buckets.

Bucket 1: Vendor Centric

The Response: *"We are already using [Competitor ABC]."*

The Reality: This is actually the easiest bucket. The prospect is *problem-aware* and *solution-aware*. You don't need to educate them on why they need to solve the problem; they are already paying money to solve it.

The Play:

Never badmouth the competitor. That is the fastest way to lose credibility. Instead, pivot to the "Gap."

1. **Validate:** *"I'm glad you're using Vendor ABC. They're a solid player in the space."*
2. **Probe for Satisfaction:** *"How has that been working out for you? Is there anything you wish it did differently?"*
3. **Position the Gap:** You know Vendor ABC is good at A and B, but misses C and D. This is your wedge.

Talk Track:

"We have a few clients who moved over from Vendor ABC. They loved them for [Feature A], but they found they were really missing [Feature C], which is where we come in. Would you be even moderately open to seeing how the two compare, just so you know what else is out there?"

Critical Step: Find out their renewal date. If they just signed a three-year contract yesterday, you can›t help them. But if they are 3-6 months out, you are perfectly timed to be the challenger.

Bucket 2: Process Centric

The Response: *"We have our own internal process for that,"* or *"We do this manually in Excel."*

The Reality: They are *problem-aware* but believe their internal «home-grown» fix is sufficient. The enemy here isn›t a competitor; it›s the **Cost of Change**. Leaders are terrified of changing processes because if the new process fails, it's on their head.

The Play:

You must highlight the Cost of Inaction. You need to show them that sticking to their current manual process is actually more expensive or risky than moving to your solution.

1. **Understand the "Why":** *"That makes sense. What made you decide to build that workflow internally?"*
2. **Highlight the Risk:** Show them what they are losing by staying manual (time, data accuracy, revenue).
3. **Safety in Change:** Assure them that the transition is safe.

Talk Track:

"I hear that a lot. It sounds like you've built a solid robust process. The reason I ask is that many leaders I speak with find that maintaining that manual process ends up costing their team about 10 hours a week in data entry—time they could spend selling. If we could automate that without disrupting your current flow, would it be worth a conversation?"

Bucket 3: Ideology Centric

The Response: *"We don't need to prioritize accounts; our top-of-funnel is fine,"* or *"We just work through the list alphabetically."*

The Reality: This is the hardest bucket. The prospect is *not* problem-aware. They have a fundamental belief (ideology) that conflicts with your premise. They think their current worldview is correct.

The Play:

You cannot pitch features here. You must pitch a New Insight. You have to break their worldview by showing them something they haven't considered.

The Talk Track (The "Insight" Pivot):

"I'm glad to hear the current approach is working. And honestly, if it's not broken, don't fix it. But did you know that typically 50-60% of the accounts on a standard sequential list aren't actually 'in-market' when you call them?

That means your team is doing a great job hitting quota working only 40% of the market. What if you could flip that, and ensure every dial was to an account showing intent? You could potentially double the pipeline with the same effort. Is that crazy to assume, or does it make some sense?"

The Goal: You want them to think, *"Huh, I never thought of it that way."* Once you shift their ideology, *then* you can sell the product.

Augment Yourself: The "Three Buckets" Prompt

You can practice this right now. Feed your specific product details into an LLM to generate these scenarios for your own role.

Copy/Paste this prompt into ChatGPT, Claude, or Gemini:

Prompt:

"You are currently acting as a [Target Persona Title, e.g., VP of Sales]. I am trying to sell you a product that solves [Problem]. Here is how we solve their problem: [Value Prop].

I cold call prospects every day, and I ask this opening question: '[Insert your opening question]'.

Can you generate three potential positive, negative, or neutral responses I might hear, one for each of these categories:

1. **Vendor Centric** (They use a competitor)
2. **Process Centric** (They do it manually or internally)
3. **Ideology Centric** (They don›t believe the problem exists)

For each response, give me a 'Consultative Pivot' script I can use to continue the conversation."

Real Roleplays for Real Objections

1. "Not Interested"

How most reps respond today:

When a prospect says, *"Not interested"*, many reps panic and immediately push back:

"What are you not interested in? I haven't told you everything yet!" Or "Thank you, have a good day" Or "Okay, no worries. I'll circle back later."

This defensive stance does two things: it signals desperation and reinforces the prospect's decision to disengage. Or they just let go of the prospect.

A better way:

Use a pattern interrupt followed by empathy.

"I figured you might say that. Honestly, I do the same when I get cold calls out of the blue. But usually, when someone tells me they're not interested, it means the timing or framing wasn't right—mind if I share in 30 seconds why others in your space decided to talk to us?"

Notice the tone—calm, human, self-aware. Instead of pressuring, you're inviting.

Another example:

You: *"I figured you'd say that. Can I level with you? I've been hearing 'not interested' a lot lately, and honestly—I say the same thing when I get cold-called out of the blue. But usually, when people say this, it's less about disinterest and more about not seeing the value yet. Can I take 30 seconds to explain why I called, and then you decide if it's worth continuing?"*

Notice how you break the autopilot response, acknowledge their feeling, and earn permission to continue

2. "Send Me an Email"

How most reps respond today:

Most SDRs reflexively ask: *"Sure, what would you like me to include?"*

Then they send a templated PDF that gets lost in the abyss of the inbox. Game over.

A better way:

Break the pattern and show empathy.

"I get it—you probably say the same thing when you get a surprise call like this. But let me ask: if I were to send something over, what's the one area you'd actually want to read about? Otherwise, I'll just become another unread email."

Another example:

They call out the elephant in the room.

You: *"I get it—I say the same thing when I get cold-called. And between us, sometimes 'send me an email' is code for 'go away you annoying sales rep.' Did I get that right?" (Chuckle)*

If they laugh or engage, you've already broken through the barrier. Then pivot:

You: *"Tell you what—give me 30 seconds to share why I reached out. If you don't think it's relevant, I'll send you some info and let you decide from there. Fair?"*

This subtle shift puts the ball back in the prospect's court. Instead of a brush-off, you've invited them to reveal what they actually care about.

3. "We're Happy with Our Current Vendor"

How most reps respond today:

They go into battle mode: *"Oh, here's how we compare against them!"* That creates resistance because the rep is attacking the buyer's past decision and gets into a feature war.

A better way:

Validate, then reframe.

"That's great—you should never stop using something that works. Most of our best customers actually said the same thing early on. If you could improve just one thing about your current setup, what would it be?"

This turns the conversation from a *defense of the vendor* into a *discussion of gaps*. Prospects often reveal where they feel pain—like reporting, integrations, or support.

Another example:

Lean into curiosity and validate the definition of "happy."

You: *"That's fantastic—any time you're seeing value from a platform, you shouldn't rush to change. Out of curiosity though, when you say you're happy, is that like 'married to them happy' or 'good enough happy'?"*

If they say married:

"Congrats. That's rare. Good on you for finding something that works. Before I let you go, what specifically makes you happy with them? I'd love to learn."

If they say good enough:

"Interesting—why just good enough? What would you improve if you could?"

This simple fork often uncovers gaps that reps can't resist talking about.

4. "We Don't Have Budget"

How most reps respond today:

The instinct is to either (a) drop the price immediately, or (b) walk away. Both responses kill long-term credibility.

A better way:

Show empathy and link to outcomes.

"Totally fair—budgets are tight everywhere right now. What we've seen, though, is that even a small pilot that improves pipeline by 10% tends to pay for itself within a quarter. Would you be open to exploring a low-lift way to test that?"

You aren't dismissing the objection—you're reframing "budget" as a question of ROI.

5. "I Don't Have Time" / "I'm Running into a Meeting"

How most reps respond today:

Most say: *"When's a better time to call?"* But the truth is, if the buyer doesn't trust you now, they won't magically trust you later.

A better way:

Acknowledge the interruption, then ask for micro-permission.

"I know you're busy—I would be too. Give me literally 30 seconds to explain why I reached out, and then you can decide if it's worth scheduling another conversation. Fair?"

This does two things: it respects their time and creates a curiosity gap. Many prospects will give you 30 seconds.

Another example:

Leverage urgency and humor.

You: *"Totally understand. Honestly, we're all too busy until we hear something that could make us less busy. Give me 30 seconds right now to explain why I called—if it's not relevant, you can hang up on me. Fair?"*

Or

You: *"I get it - I say the same when I get cold-called out of the blue. And I'm getting the feeling that's just your polite way of saying "Go away you annoying sales rep!" - Did I get that right?" (Chuckle)*

You'll be surprised how many times prospects actually agree to talk post this! Be mindful that they might really be heading to a meeting as well. Avoid asking any more questions if there's resistance beyond this point.

6. "We Already Have Compliance / Audit Covered"

(Let's dive deeper with a targeted example. Say you're selling a compliance software handling SOC2 / GDPR etc.)

How most reps respond today:

They dismiss it with, *"Well, we're different,"* or dive into a feature dump.

A better way:

Use curiosity.

"That's great—most companies I speak with already have compliance frameworks in place. What I often hear though is that teams spend hours manually collecting evidence or chasing auditors for clarifications. Curious, how are you managing that today?"

Instead of contradicting, you've invited them to reveal inefficiencies hidden beneath the surface.

7. "How Much Does It Cost?"

How most reps respond today:

They blurt out the price with no context. The prospect, who has no anchoring yet, thinks it's too expensive right off the bat.

A better way:

Delay price until you've built value.

"Great question. Pricing depends heavily on scope, which we haven't discussed yet. I don't want to do you a disservice by giving you a number without context. Could I ask a couple of quick questions to understand your situation better?"

This keeps control in your hands while signaling transparency.

8. "Just Send Me Some Info"

How most reps respond today:

They say: *"Sure, I'll send you a deck."* Then it goes unread.

A better way:

Reframe the ask into a conversation.

"I'd be happy to do that, but in my experience, when I send info blindly it doesn't hit the mark. If you give me a minute to ask a couple of questions, I can send something that's actually relevant. Deal?"

Here, you're turning a passive "brush-off" into an active dialogue.

9. "Not on the Roadmap"

What most reps say today:

"Okay, I'll check back next quarter." (Another entry in the "call me later" graveyard.)

A better way:

Challenge with curiosity.

You: *"Totally understand. Just so I know—when you say not on the roadmap, is that because your customers aren't* *asking for it, or because you don't [converse of your product philosophy] way? The reason I ask is that teams sometimes underestimate how much this slows their sales cycle. If a customer asked you tomorrow about X or Y, how would you handle that today?"*

This shifts the focus from "not a priority" to "what happens when it becomes urgent."

10. "I'm Not the Right Person" / "I'm Not the Decision Maker"

What most reps say today:

"Oh okay, who's the right person then?" (And now you're sent into the black hole of referrals.)

A better way:

Secure a warm intro.

You: *"Got it—thanks for being upfront. Would you be open to writing a quick email intro with me CC'd? I can send you a draft after this call to make it easier. You know how it is—if I just cold-email them, I'll be ignored. If it comes from you, it makes this so much smoother. I promise I won't spam them like a pesky salesperson."*

This tactic turns dead ends into doors.

The AI Advantage

If you truly want to be augmented—not replaced—you need to think of AI not as a crutch, but as a sparring partner. It's not about outsourcing your skills. It's about sharpening them until you're sharper than the rep who never trains.

How augmented reps practice differently:

- **Pattern Recognition at Scale**
  AI can analyze hundreds of your calls in minutes, tagging which objections come up most often, and which responses consistently lead to meetings instead of dead ends. Imagine having a personal coach who remembers every single mistake you've ever made, and shows you how to fix it—that's augmentation.

- **AI Roleplay for Reps**
  Most reps practice live, on their prospects (a dangerous way to learn). Use AI to roleplay 20 objections in 20 minutes with AI tools like Hyperbound or even ChatGPT. They get their reps in before the game starts. Think of it like a fighter shadowboxing before a match—you're warmed up before you ever step in.

- **Talk Tracks**
  Humans default to the same 3–4 lines when under pressure. AI can generate 15 variations of your

objection response so you don't sound like every other rep reading a script. You keep the authenticity, but you bring fresh angles that surprise the prospect and sound like a human, not like a bank teller selling credit cards everyday!

But here's the truth: AI can't replace empathy, tone, or timing. It can prepare you, but only you can deliver trust in the moment. Augmentation means AI fills the gaps in speed and repetition, while you step into the role only a human can play.

AI can help you practice. Only you can perform.

Welcome Objections

The goal is not to **eliminate objections**. That's impossible. The goal is to **welcome them**—because objections mean your prospect is still in the conversation. Ghosts don't object.

Top 1% SDRs and AEs treat objections like open doors disguised as barriers. They don't fight. They don't fold. They listen, reframe, and redirect—toward the meeting, not the argument.

And as AI gets smarter, the margin between good and great will shrink. Anyone can generate a decent response with a tool. But only the reps who **combine AI's speed with human empathy** will stay irreplaceable.

By now, you've seen how every objection tells a story — not of resistance, but of reasoning. Here, we broke down real-world objections from cold calls and discovery conversations, learning how to uncover what the buyer truly means when they say "not now" or "we already have something." But while objection handling sharpens your ability to respond, the next level of selling is about anticipation — seeing connections before the buyer even voices them.

That's what *Joining the Dots* is all about.

In the next chapter, we'll move from reacting to predicting, from answering questions to building intelligent, creative angles that make your outreach feel deeply relevant. You'll learn how top reps use context, signals, and human judgment to form powerful points of view that AI alone can't replicate.

CHAPTER 8

JOINING THE DOTS

What Does "Joining the Dots" Mean?

AI can parse signals. Humans can connect them. That's the difference between a line of data and a line that lands in someone's inbox with a smile, a nod, or curiosity. Too many outreach attempts are built on forced premises: "You raised funding, so you must want X." Buyers feel this instantly. It reads like someone dragging and dropping their LinkedIn headline into a template.

Before we dive into scenarios and examples, let's pause and really define what "joining the dots" means in sales.

In essence, it's the human skill of connecting scattered signals into a meaningful *point of view* (POV) or angle. An expansion announcement, a CEO's LinkedIn post, a sudden hiring spree, a podcast comment—individually, these are just dots. On their own, they're raw signals. The job of a modern seller is not to dump those signals into a template but to *interpret* them. To turn them into context, narrative, and relevance that resonates with another human being.

This is exactly where humans still hold an edge over AI. AI is getting very good at finding dots like funding events, role changes, technology installs, but it often fails at weaving those dots into a coherent story. It tends to default to surface-level logic: "You raised funding, so you must need growth tools." That's not wrong, but it's not compelling either. It misses the emotional driver, the nuance, the subtle contradictions that make a message feel *thoughtful* instead of *mechanical.*

Angles are what make the difference. Without the right angle, even the most beautifully worded message will fall flat. Think of angles as the *premise* of your outreach: the underlying reason why this person, at this company, at this time, should even bother giving you 30 seconds of attention. It's not about being clever for the sake of it. It's about being intentional.

Prospects love to correct us more than they love to agree with us. If you come in with a firm statement—"You must be struggling with X"—they'll instinctively resist. But if you frame your angle as a hypothesis—"I imagine expanding to London could create payroll complexity because…"—they lean in. They don't feel sold to; they feel invited to clarify.

So the point of this chapter is not to hand you plug-and-play scripts. It's to train your *thinking*. To show you how to construct angles with a simple methodology that blends personal empathy with account realities.

Building Premises

The premise (or "hook") is the most important part of building a relationship. The depth of the premise determines whether you build a relationship or get lost in the sea of everyday cold emails. Think of it as the opening riff of a song — it has to catch the ear before the lyrics even matter.

There are three primary kinds of premises:

1. Building Premises with Personal Words

Use the prospect's *own language* as the launchpad.

- Example: A prospect posts, "I'm tired of wasting time on unqualified leads."

You could use: *"Correct me if I'm wrong, but you've mentioned you hate the time sink of unqualified leads. What if you could filter them out without adding steps to your team's workflow?"*

By echoing their words, you make it difficult for them to dismiss you — because you're not guessing, you're reflecting.

2. Building premises with Observed Interests

Prospect signals something unique in their profile or posts.

- Example: "Weekend salsa dancer" in their headline.

You could use an analogy: *"If only prospecting could feel like salsa — smooth, rhythmic, and without missed steps. Curious how you're enabling your reps to hit that flow today?"*

It's light, but human, and transitions naturally into business.

3. Building premises with Contextual Relevance

Tie signals into their current business stage.

- Example: *"With your Series B round, it looks like expanding into enterprise is on the roadmap. The tricky part we see is balancing bigger deals with cycle times. How are you thinking about that trade-off?"*

This is good but lacks personalization depth. Nevertheless, it's a start to learning and building meaningful premises.

Each hook is about showing *intentionality*. You're proving: *"I didn't send this to a hundred people. I did my homework. You're not just a name on my list!"*

Let's take a look at some real-life examples that I have personally encountered.

Scenario 1: Selling payroll software to an HR Director

Signals observed:

- The company announced expansion from the U.S. into London.
- Open roles for HR generalists and finance coordinators in London.

Possible angles for different internal products:

1. **Payroll module** → Expanding into London means the HR team now needs to navigate UK employment laws, cross-border payroll regulations, and local tax codes. Without proper systems, compliance risks and payroll errors can quickly spiral.
2. **Onboarding module** → Every new office brings a flood of fresh hires who need smooth first days. If onboarding is clunky, new employees start disengaged, which damages both morale and retention.
3. **Employee experience module** → Pay accuracy and timeliness are directly tied to trust. A single mistake in a new market can cause employees to lose confidence in leadership. Protecting morale during expansion is as critical as compliance.

Prioritization: Payroll module takes top priority. Why? Compliance risk is the most immediate, unavoidable pain point when entering a new geography. Onboarding and morale matter, but if paychecks are wrong, everything else collapses.

Scenario 2: Selling a cybersecurity platform to a CTO

Signals observed:

- The company just partnered with a major cloud provider.
- CTO posted: "Innovation should never lag behind compliance."

Possible angles for different internal products:

1. **Cloud security module** → Moving workloads to a new cloud provider increases the attack surface. Without enhanced controls, innovation could stall under the weight of new vulnerabilities.
2. **Governance/compliance dashboards** → The CTO's own words highlight compliance as a central theme. Dashboards that prove compliance without slowing teams directly match this belief.
3. **Vendor consolidation** → Partnerships often introduce tool sprawl. Offering a single pane of glass reduces stack complexity while still scaling securely.

Prioritization: Governance module takes top priority. Why? You always lead with the executive's stated belief. Their "innovation vs compliance" comment tells you exactly what's keeping them up at night. Cloud workloads are real, but compliance-first is their framing. This might seem counterintuitive with the fact that cloud security might top it but the art of sales is figuring out what keeps the CTO at night that AI tends to miss.

Scenario 3: Selling a sales acceleration suite to a VP of Sales

Signals observed:

- The company just raised **$50M in Series C funding**.
- They've opened **80+ SDR/AE roles** on their careers page.
- In a recent interview, the VP said: *"We spend a lot of time making sure we target the right accounts."*

Possible angles for different internal products

- **Lead scoring module** → On the surface, it looks like they already prioritize account selection heavily. But that phrasing — *"we spend a lot of time"* — is a clue. It signals a *resource drain*. You could position your lead scoring as a way to keep quality high *without the heavy lift*. It's not about fixing broken targeting, it's about giving them back hours.
- **Territory planning module** → If their reps are manually spending so much effort on targeting, how

are they going to manage equitable coverage when 80 new reps come in? Territory balancing becomes an even bigger headache when the team's targeting process is already consuming bandwidth.

- **Manager insights module** → Spending so much time targeting means managers probably have less time for coaching and performance oversight. Surfacing patterns on which reps are making good targeting choices could lighten their load.

Prioritization: The strongest angle to lead with here is the **lead scoring module**, not because the VP doubts their ability to choose the right accounts, but because of the hidden cost embedded in their own words. Saying *"we spend a lot of time"* signals pride, but it also signals inefficiency. The more time reps and managers pour into account selection, the less time they have for actual selling. That time cost becomes an invisible tax on growth, especially with 80+ new hires coming on board.

Scenario 4: Selling a marketing automation platform to a VP of Marketing

Signals observed:

- In a podcast interview, the VP casually mentioned: *"Our team spends more time stitching together reports than actually planning campaigns."*

- On the company's careers page, three new marketing ops roles were posted, all emphasizing *"cross-platform analytics experience."*
- On LinkedIn, the VP posted: *"Simplicity is the future of Martech."*
- They also shared an article: *"Why Martech Sprawl is the Silent Killer of Creativity."*

Possible angles for different internal products:

- **Campaign Planner** → The VP's own frustration is about lost time. A campaign planner reframes the problem: if reporting didn't consume the day, their team could finally get back to building campaigns that drive revenue.
- **Integration Hub** → The deeper problem isn't reporting itself, but why reporting is broken: martech sprawl. An integration hub unifies their stack, aligns with their belief in simplicity, and stops creativity from being buried under complexity.
- **Adoption Analytics** → With three new AI tools in six months, adoption isn't guaranteed. Analytics expose what's delivering ROI, what's shelfware, and where budgets are leaking.

Prioritization:

Campaign Planner solves the *surface pain* — the VP and their team are frustrated with how reporting eats into planning. It's very human, very immediate. When the VP says "simplicity," they're not just making a philosophical statement. They're voicing a leadership principle: complexity is choking creativity. Tool sprawl is the operational proof of that. The Integration Hub is the clearest bridge between their philosophy and their operations. It's not just about reporting efficiency — it's about bringing their entire Martech stack back into alignment with their vision.

How to think about prioritization

- If you want to mirror the VP's personal frustration (reporting > planning), you'd lead with Campaign Planner.
- If you want to mirror the VP's leadership philosophy (simplicity > sprawl), you'd lead with Integration Hub.

Both are valid, but one resonates at the *individual operator pain level*, while the other resonates at the *strategic leadership level.*

The art is deciding which angle to lead with, based on the context of your outreach. In an email where you want to hook relevance quickly, **Campaign Planner** might win. In a boardroom conversation where the VP is thinking long-term, **Integration Hub** might dominate.

Scenario 6: Selling an AI coding tool to a CTO

Signals observed:

- In a conference keynote, the CTO said: *"The hardest part isn't hiring developers, it's keeping them focused on solving core business problems instead of boilerplate."*
- On the company's GitHub, several repos show recent commits from contractors on repetitive refactoring and documentation updates.
- The careers page highlights a push for full-stack engineers with "speed and adaptability" as key requirements.
- On LinkedIn, the CTO shared a post about burnout among engineering teams and the need to "reduce cognitive load."

Possible angles for different internal products:

- **Code Autocompletion/AI Pair Programming** → The keynote itself reveals the CTO's north star: freeing devs from boilerplate. Autocompletion that accelerates routine coding directly maps to that frustration.
- **Automated Refactoring Module** → GitHub commits from contractors working on repetitive refactors is a subtle but strong signal. Automating those tasks means

senior engineers reclaim focus for innovation rather than maintenance.

- **Documentation Generator** → Burnout and cognitive load tie back to context switching. If docs are auto-generated and always current, developers spend less mental energy maintaining knowledge hygiene.

Prioritization:

The **refactoring module** edges out as the top play here. Why? Because it speaks to a pain already costing the company money (contractors doing low-leverage tasks) and time (senior devs distracted from core work). While boilerplate and burnout matter, those are abstract problems until they hit budgets and delivery schedules. Refactoring is the visible drag on productivity — and solving it creates instant credibility with the CTO. Once you address that, you can expand into autocompletion and documentation as natural next steps.

The Framework for Joining the Dots

Think of this like building a case. Every case needs evidence (signals), an angle (your POV), and a lead (the single, sharp line you'll actually put in front of your prospect).

Step 1. Collect Your Signals

Start wide. Pull in as many signals as you can across **four buckets**:

1. **Personal signals** → things the prospect said, wrote, or shared. (Posts, interviews, bios.)
2. **Account signals** → company-level events. (Funding, expansion, layoffs, partnerships.)
3. **Functional signals** → how their department operates. (Job postings, tech stack, org changes.)
4. **Industry signals** → outside pressures shaping their world. (Regulation, market shifts, competitor moves.)

Step 2. Draft Multiple Angles

For each set of signals, ask: *"What story does this data point want to tell?"* Don't settle for the obvious one. Try three to four different POVs. Example:

- A funding round could angle toward expansion, risk management, or talent acquisition — not just "congrats."
- A LinkedIn post on burnout could angle toward efficiency, retention, or tooling.

Step 3. Stress-Test Your Angles

Now comes the human part — judgment. For each possible angle, ask:

- *Does this tie back to a problem they feel today (not six months from now)?*
- *Is this angle anchored in their own words or actions, not just my assumptions?*
- *Does this angle lead naturally into one product/module I can credibly position?*

Step 4. Prioritize the Lead

Here's the trap most reps fall into: trying to pitch everything at once. Don't. The best messages are simple. Choose **one angle to lead with**, and here's how to decide:

1. **Executive voice wins.** If the buyer themselves said something (podcast, post, quote), that belief takes priority.
2. **Follow the money.** If a signal shows actual cost (contractors, wasted spend, hiring strain), that often outweighs philosophical signals.
3. **Remove the bottleneck.** If several signals point to problems, pick the one that's preventing everything else from working. (E.g., integration before orchestration.)

Step 5. Park the Rest for Later

The other angles aren't wasted. They're your follow-up ammo. If the lead angle doesn't land, you can pivot without sounding repetitive.

A Simple Template to Think With

Whenever you're sitting with a new account, walk yourself through this checklist:

- **Signals observed:** [list everything you see — personal, account, functional, industry]
- **Possible angles:** [write at least 2–3 ways you could connect these dots to your product]
- **Prioritization:** [pick one to lead with — and explain to yourself why it matters most *now*]

That's it. If you just run this loop every time, you'll always lead with the sharpest point instead of a spray of guesses.

Using AI to Augment Yourself

Here's how AI fits into each step of the framework you just learned:

1. **Signal Collection**
    - AI can surface the flood of raw signals on personal, account functional and industry related signals
    - Make sure that you use tools that can capture fresh, real-time signals instead of importing data from stale databases.
    - Without this raw material and data recency, you have nothing to join together.

2. Angle Generation

- Prompt AI to bucket signals into *Highly Relevant*, *Moderately Relevant*, and *Less Relevant*.
- Example prompt:

"You are a research analyst at [company]. Your job is to rank the following signals in three buckets based on how relevant they are for writing a meaningful outbound email to a VP of Marketing."

- This saves you the manual effort of differentiating the noise from the real signals.

3. Hypothesis Framing

- Use AI to draft multiple POV options. Don't accept them blindly, instead look at them as rough sketches.

4. Prioritization

- This step is 100% human. AI cannot tell you what keeps the CTO awake at night or what matters most to the VP of Marketing.
- You decide which product module or angle deserves the lead. One strong, simple angle will always beat three scattered ones.

5. Message Drafting

- Once you've picked the angle, AI can draft variations of the message in different tones, lengths, or formats (email, LinkedIn DM, call opener).
- Use meta-prompting to templatize this so you're not starting from scratch each time.

Joining the Dots was about developing the mental muscle behind great outreach — the ability to read signals, connect them with context, and form intelligent points of view. But ideas alone don't open conversations. The real test begins when you try to translate those insights into words that make someone stop, think, and respond.

That's where we move next.

In *Writing Emails Like a Human*, we shift from thought to expression, from identifying what matters to communicating it in a way that feels natural and real. This chapter isn't about templates or frameworks; it's about writing in a way that reflects empathy, judgment, and timing, the very things that make humans irreplaceable in an AI-driven world.

CHAPTER 9

WRITING EMAILS LIKE A HUMAN

In the last chapter, we saw how to merge signals and join the dots to design outreach that feels relevant. Now, let's tackle one of the most over-used yet still critical channels in sales: email.

Yes, we've heard the prophecy for years—"email is dead." And yet, in 2025, your prospects are still checking their inbox daily. The truth? Emails are not dead. Bad emails are dead. If you write like a robot, you'll be ignored. But if you write like a human, you will get replies.

This chapter isn't about tricks or templates. It's about rewriting the DNA of your cold emails so they *stand out in an AI-saturated world.*

The Email Landscape in 2025

Today, a new generation of tools—Clay, Instantly, Smartlead, and even the emerging "AI SDRs"—make it easy to send highly targeted email sequences at scale.

These platforms are excellent at building workflows and capturing signals like:

- Roles and positions a company is hiring for
- Events the company attended
- Leadership changes
- New product launches
- Compliance news or regulatory shifts
- Revenue growth
- Recent funding rounds
- Language on their website
- Customer reviews on platforms like G2

All of these signals create **relevance.** And relevance is powerful. But relevance alone does not equal personalization.

These platforms have gotten frighteningly good. Which means your real competition isn't just other humans—it's machines.

So how do you win? By showing the *one thing* AI cannot fake: judgment, empathy, and true relevance.

Relevance vs. Personalization (Or Both?)

Relevance is when you use signals that show awareness of the company's context. Personalization is when you show the prospect that your message could not have been generated by a workflow or an AI engine.

True personalization doesn't come from scraped details like where someone went to school or what city they live in. That's shallow and meaningless. Instead, **good personalization comes from using a prospect's own self-written words and emotional cues.**

Look at what they've posted on LinkedIn, the content they've written, or the topics they repeatedly engage with. Notice what excites them, what frustrates them, and what motivates them. That's where the human advantage lies.

The best part? This goldmine of context is often locked away from scrapers. LinkedIn posts, personal takes, and subtle emotional signals are much harder for automation tools to capture. Which means *you* can lean into them.

So here's the formula:

- **Relevance is good.**
- **Timing + Relevance + Personalization is unbeatable.**

And if you're stuck with a prospect who has no visible footprint? That's the "curse of data." In those cases, don't force bad personalization—fall back on account-level signals and lean more heavily on **cold calls** to build authentic rapport.

Timing: The Missing Third Dimension

We've all heard the two pillars of great outbound: **relevance** and **personalization**.

But there's a third element that's often ignored and it quietly decides whether any of your outreach will even matter. That element is **timing**.

Think of timing as the silent multiplier. You can write the most relevant, perfectly personalized message in the world, but if your prospect isn't *ready* to care, it's like showing up to a birthday party a week late with the best cake in town.

Still a great cake. Still no one there to eat it.

What Timing Really Means

Timing isn't just *when* you send the email.

It's *whether* the account or person is in the right headspace, business phase, or operational window to even look at what you're offering.

Here's an easy analogy:

Imagine you've just bought the brand-new iPhone 17 Pro.

Now Samsung offers you its latest flagship at **50% off**.

Would you buy it? Probably not. Not because it's irrelevant — the offer's amazing, but because you're *not in market.*

That's timing.

It's not about whether the product fits you, it's about whether *now* is the right moment for you to even think about it.

The Difference Between Personalization, Relevance, and Timing

Most sales books stop at *relevance* and *personalization*, but they miss how *timing* acts as the invisible backbone that determines *when and why* something finally clicks for a buyer.

Think of it like this:

Layer	Question It Answers	What It Reflects	Who It's About
Personalization	"Do you know me?"	Micro signals — words, tone, preferences, identity	The *individual*
Relevance	"Do you understand my world?"	Macro signals — company stage, market, initiatives	The *organization*
Timing	"Do you understand *why now*?"	Contextual inflection points — readiness, pressure, and sequence of events	The *moment*

Avoiding the Obvious

The blueprint most automation tools follow is predictable:

- Observation → Problem → Value Proposition → Social Proof → CTA

  or

- Observation → Problem → Agitate → CTA → P.S.

That's why so many emails feel interchangeable. Your job is to break that pattern and make your email feel like it was written by someone who actually thought about the prospect.

Let's look at some examples of stating the obvious v/s not.

Funding Signals

Cliché opener:

"Hey John, congrats on the recent round of funding."

Sounds polite and nice, but let's be real—are you actually celebrating their fundraising success? You know within your heart that it translates to: *"You've got money now, can I have some?"*

Prospects know this, and it wastes valuable space.

Better approach:

"Hey John, with your recent Series B, it looks like moving up-market is now a priority—Mike even called it out in your press release."

This doesn't state the obvious. It goes straight to the meaningful context and shows you're paying attention.

Hiring Signals

Cliché opener:

"Hey Sarah, I saw you're hiring SDRs—congrats on growing the team!"

Prospects see through this. It's the most overused automation template.

Better approach:

"Hey Sarah, with adding five SDRs, I'm guessing leadership is doubling down on human-led outbound and not the AI SDR route."

That single shift moves that note from shallow observation to a higher-level business insight.

Event Attendance

Cliché opener:

"Hi Mark, I saw you were at Dreamforce. How was the event?"

Every rep who scrapes the attendee list will send the same note.

Better approach:

"Hi Mark, saw you spoke at Dreamforce about the shift to PLG & mentioned pipeline coverage being the hardest part to forecast…"

This shows you didn't just see their name on a list—you paid attention to what they said.

Leadership Change

Cliché opener:

"Hi Alex, congrats on your new role as CMO at Acme!"

Again—obvious, impersonal, and feels like a LinkedIn bot.

Better approach:

"Hi Alex, I'm guessing you're rethinking about deploying your playbook from ABC at Acme as the new CMO in a new context with quick impact…"

Now you're relevant to their actual day-to-day reality.

Product Launch

Cliché opener:

"Hey Lisa, congrats on the new product launch!"

Empty calories—it doesn't spark a reply.

Better approach:

"Hey Lisa, with launching 4 major features this month, it probably takes your reps a few weeks to learn and position…"

Here, you reframe the launch as a doorway into a problem space you solve.

Compliance / Security Signal

Cliché opener:

"Hi James, I saw your company just got SOC2 compliant. That's awesome!"

It's factual, but it doesn't lead anywhere.

Better approach:

"Hi James, I'm guessing you're gearing up for moving up market with the recent SOC2 compliance…"

This shows insight into what comes after the milestone.

Customer Review / Reputation Signal

Cliché opener:

"Hi Priya, I saw your company got a lot of great G2 reviews lately. Congrats!"

Again—shallow, doesn't sound like you care.

Better approach:

"Hi Priya, read your G2 and noticed customers love your support team, but a few mentioned reporting is clunky."

Now you're anchoring in the customer's reality, not just the company's PR.

Website Language / Messaging

Cliché opener:

"Hi Daniel, I was on your site and saw you help companies with [generic phrase from their homepage]. That's really interesting!"

It's lazy—it sounds like you copy-pasted.

Better approach:

"Hi Daniel, your website emphasizes 'expanding internationally' as a key priority. Usually, that makes revenue ops messy—multiple currencies..."

This turns their own language into a meaningful question.

Signals by themselves create **relevance**. They tell you *why* you should be reaching out and *what* the context is. But signals combined with **empathy and thoughtful framing** create **personalization**—the kind of communication that feels like it could only have come from you, not from a sequence builder or workflow engine.

Here's the subtle but powerful shift: don't go into your outreach with rigid premises. Instead, go in with **educated guesses**. Prospects love correcting us when we're slightly off, but they tend to resist outright when we sound too certain from the start. That's the psychology of engagement.

When you write, frame your message as if you're piecing together what *might* be happening in their world, not dictating what is. That way, even if you miss the mark, the prospect is more likely to respond with, *"Not exactly—we're actually doing X instead."* And just like that, you've sparked a real conversation.

In other words:

- **Relevance** gets you noticed.
- **Personalization** earns you a response.
- **Guesses, not premises**, open the door to dialogue instead of resistance.

This is the art of writing emails like a human in the AI age.

Diagnosing Objections in Writing

Every outbound email lives at the crossroads of **two possible objections**. Get this diagnosis right, and you're in the game. Get it wrong, and your carefully crafted outreach evaporates into silence.

Current State Objection – "Not urgent enough right now"

What it sounds like in writing:

- "We're focused on other priorities this quarter."
- "Budget is tight until next year."
- "Check back in Q3."

Translation: They acknowledge the problem but don't feel it's painful enough to act *today*.

Example scenario:

A VP of Sales knows their reps are missing quota because forecasting is inaccurate. But leadership has already locked the budget this quarter for a CRM migration. They'll nod at your point but won't move yet.

How to address in an email:

Instead of hammering ROI (which they already conceptually accept), lean into the cost **of waiting** framed in terms of momentum lost.

"I know budget is locked this quarter. What stood out though is your team is onboarding 15 new AEs in Q2. If they inherit the same forecasting gaps, the cost of inaction isn't just one more quarter—it compounds with every new rep you bring in."

You're not fighting the objection. You're reframing why *now* matters.

Future State Objection – "We're not sure you're the right partner"

What it sounds like in writing:

- "We're still evaluating different vendors."
- "Need to confirm internally if this is the right fit."
- "We'll revisit after comparing options."

Translation: They *do* believe the problem is urgent but don't yet believe **you** are the safest or smartest bet.

Example scenario:

A Head of Marketing agrees attribution is a mess and has the budget approved. But she's wary—three vendors claim to fix it, and her team is testing two pilots already.

How to address in an email:

Don't double down on urgency. They already feel it. Instead, de-risk the decision and build credibility.

"I saw you're already exploring attribution platforms. Teams we work with at HubSpot and Segment told us their biggest worry early on wasn't features—it was how fast their teams could adopt it. Would it help if I shared how they cut ramp time from six months to under two?"

Notice: you're not pushing. You're *validating their caution* and offering social proof tied to adoption risk.

Why this distinction matters

- **Misdiagnosis #1:** Pitching ROI to a current state objection.

  → They'll agree in theory but defer in practice.
- **Misdiagnosis #2:** Pitching cost of inaction to a future state objection.

→ They'll nod ("yes, we know it's urgent") but still won't pick you.

Reps lose months here by sending the right message to the wrong objection.

Before you hit send, ask yourself:

1. Is my prospect likely to think the *problem isn't big enough yet*? → Lead with **why waiting costs more than acting now**.
2. Or are they thinking *we're not sure you're the right solution*? → Lead with **credibility, adoption, and de-risking with evidence**.

Outbound becomes far less about a clever turn of phrase and far more about really diagnosing the problem at its core.

The Eternal Question: What to Include (and What Not To)

After talking to 654+ reps, the #1 question they ask is *"How to construct an outbound email?"* One of the biggest traps sales reps fall into is **analysis paralysis** when writing emails quickly. The questions pile up fast:

- Should I add a case study?
- Should I tell a story?
- Should I make it funny?
- Should I embed a video?
- Should I keep it under 50 words? And so on…

The truth? **There's no universal formula.** The single best test we have all been taught is this:

Would I reply to this if I were the prospect?

Sounds simple. But here's where the problem actually arises: now instead of thinking like the buyer, we customize the email to match **our own style**. That's dangerous because buyers aren't us. Buyers have their own triggers, motivations, and blind spots.

The Funny Email That Fell Flat

I remember Jake (obviously fictitious), a new SDR, was extremely witty. Every email he wrote included a clever joke or a pun. His emails to a CFO of a manufacturing firm:

"Looks like you've been crunching numbers harder than my grandma crunches cookies."

Jake thought he nailed it. But the CFO? Not amused. In fact, the CFO replied as "unprofessional and stupid"

What makes *you* laugh doesn't always land with someone else—especially someone who spends their day managing risk, compliance, and budgets. I'm not saying humor is bad, but it must be carefully aligned with the prospect's personality as well.

The Long Case Study That Buried the Hook

Sarah had a great client story—a Fortune 500 company that doubled productivity using her product. She decided to include this amazing **case study** in her email.

The prospect didn't even finish reading. They skimmed, missed the key point, and deleted it.

I'm not saying case studies don't work. How can you be sure that your prospect is actually interested in one though?

The job isn't to show how clever, funny, or knowledgeable you are—it's also to **meet the buyer in their emotional frame**. That's why understanding prospect psychology is such a breakthrough in the age of AI: it helps you adapt the *tone* of the same message for a CFO, a Head of Marketing, or a VP of Engineering.

So the next time you ask yourself, *"Should I add a joke, a story, or a case study?"* flip the question:

"Would this buyer, with this personality, at this moment, actually care?"

If the answer is no, cut it. If yes, keep it lean. Because in today's inbox, **clarity beats cleverness, and empathy beats templates.**

You can use LeadLabs, Crystal or Humantic to lean into understanding prospect psychology in a click.

Writing Worthy Subject Lines

If your subject line doesn't earn attention, nothing else in your email matters.

It's the doorman to your message, and in a world where every inbox feels like Times Square, your subject line has one second to decide whether it's getting in or getting swiped into the SPAM folder.

We've all been there: you craft the perfect email, refine every word, find the perfect call to action—and then watch it die unopened. The culprit? Possibly a lazy or overused subject line.

The Problem with "Personalized" Subject Lines

Most reps think they're personalizing when they drop a prospect's name or company name into the subject line. On paper, it sounds smart. In practice, it screams *marketing automation.*

Think about it, who usually puts your name in a subject line? Not your friends or colleagues. It's Uber:

"Vineeth, your ride is waiting."

Or a food delivery app:

"What's for dinner tonight, Vineeth?"

These patterns have trained our brains to instantly classify name-based subject lines as *promotions*. And once that mental filter kicks in, your email is halfway to the Promotions tab or to the Spam.

So instead of trying to sound "personalized," your goal is to sound *familiar*. You want the prospect's brain to go, *Wait, is this from someone I know?* That's what gets your emails opened.

Make It Sound Like an Internal Email

The most opened emails in any company aren't from customers or vendors, they're from colleagues. They have the most boring subject lines imaginable:

"Q4 analysis."

"Deck."

"PDF update."

No emojis. No "quick question." No forced cleverness. Just plain, direct, *human.*

That's your first and simplest hack: **make your email sound like it came from inside their company.** If your subject line could believably appear in their internal inbox, you've already won the first battle.

Pattern Interrupts: Making People Stop

Now, not every subject line should blend in. Sometimes you want to *break* the pattern. That's where "pattern-interrupt" subject lines come in, the ones that make people pause mid-scroll and think, *"What on earth is this?*

Something like:

"Chocolate monkey."

"Swimming butterfly."

These work because they *don't* make sense—until they do. They create enough intrigue to earn a click, but they only work if the body of your email connects the dots. Otherwise, it's clickbait.

So if your email later mentions a "butterfly effect" of productivity or a "sweet spot" in hiring, suddenly "Chocolate monkey" doesn't feel random, it feels intentional and creative.

The rule here is simple: **write your email first**, then look back and pick two unusual yet relevant words that appear inside it. Combine them into a subject line that interrupts—but still belongs.

Example:

"60% payroll."

Weird? Yes. But if the email talks about how your software improved a client's payroll accuracy by 60%, it instantly makes sense. And that curiosity buys you the open.

The Emotion Hook: Speaking to What They Feel, Not What They Do

Another underrated approach is emotional subject lines, the ones that connect on a human level. These aren't about cleverness, they're about *resonance.*

If a prospect's LinkedIn headline says "Dad of three" or they post about morning runs with their dog, use that as emotional context. A subject line like:

"Morning Run"

"Cooper" (The Dog's name)

...doesn't just say "I did my research." It says, *I see you as a person, not a pipeline.*

These lines feel one-to-one. They cut through automation fatigue. And that's really the whole goal: to prove that your email **could not have come from an automated campaign.** The more it feels handcrafted, the higher your odds of getting a response.

Best Practices for Writing Subject Lines That Get Opened

- **Keep it under three words.** Brevity signals confidence and avoids truncation on mobile.
- **Avoid over-polish.** Perfect grammar and capitalization feel corporate. Lowercase or simple fragments feel real.
- **Write it *after* the email.** The body gives you context and keywords for better hooks.
- **Match tone to intent.** If the email feels internal, keep it direct. If it's creative, play with tension.
- **Test emotional vs. pattern-interrupt lines.** Different prospects respond to different triggers—no one size fits all.

The Real Purpose of a Subject Line

The subject line isn't about cleverness—it's about being simple and **earning curiosity.** It's your one-line audition for attention.

If your prospect believes, even for a second, that a human wrote this email just for them, you've earned the right to start a conversation. If not, your message joins the endless graveyard of unread emails in "Promotions."

So before you hit send, ask yourself:

"Does this sound like it came from a colleague… or a campaign?"

If it sounds like the latter, go back and rewrite it. Because in modern outreach, the first impression isn't your pitch, it's your subject line.

Practical Workflow with AI

So how do you use AI without outsourcing your brain? Here's a framework I've used (and refined) with real teams:

1. Signal Ranking Prompt

Instead of drowning in noise, start by asking AI to rank signals.

"You are a research analyst at Acme Corp. Here's what we do at Acme Corp: [Value Prop]

Rank signals for outreach to [various personas]. Bucket them as Highly relevant, Moderately relevant, Less relevant."

This forces clarity. Instead of treating every scrap of intel as gold, you now have a prioritized shortlist.

2. Enrich Signals with Research

AI on its own is surface-level. Take the ranked signals and run them through Perplexity or a search engine. If "expanding to Europe" is flagged as highly relevant, dig deeper: Which markets? How soon? Who's leading the expansion?

3. Capture Prospect-Level Signals in Real Time

Here's where most AI breaks. ChatGPT, Claude and Perplexity can't pull yesterday's LinkedIn post because it's not indexed on the public web yet. That's where tools like LeadLabs shine. They'll surface things like:

- Prospect just posted about struggling to fill SDR seats.
- VP of Marketing shared frustration about attribution models.

That's the difference between writing "Congrats on funding" and "Sucks how attribution models are…"

4. Meta-Prompting

You don't have to be an expert in prompting. Don't overthink "prompt engineering". Start messy:

"Help me write a cold email to a VP of Sales about why hiring more SDRs won't fix connect rates."

Then ask AI to templatize it:

"You are an expert prompt engineer. Your goal is to rewrite my prompt as a reusable API prompt and templatize it with variables like {prospect_name}, {signal}, {pain_point}."

Now you have a repeatable, scalable workflow you can plug into a custom GPT etc. We will cover more on Meta Prompting in Chapter 10.

5. Automate Variables

But passing variables manually kills momentum because it takes a bunch of time for each prospect. You can either ask your custom GPT, Clay etc. to act as a research agent and fill up all the variables by itself or you could use tools like LeadLabs that can push real-time prospect signals (a few minutes old) straight into your prompts.

Data – The Silent Killer

Sales reps are often told to "own their outcomes." If a prospect doesn't reply to an email, the instinct is to blame yourself: *"Maybe my subject line was weak. Maybe my CTA wasn't sharp enough. Maybe I should have personalized more."* And yes—sometimes those things are true. But here's a reality that almost no sales manager admits out loud

"Sometimes it's not you. Sometimes, it's just the data."

Bad or outdated data is the *silent killer* of outbound performance. You could spend 15-20 minutes crafting the most thoughtful email, with a meaningful premise and a thought provoking CTA, but if the underlying data is wrong—it just won't matter because the boat has already sailed.

If the person no longer works at the company, if their title has changed, if the funding announcement you're referencing happened six months ago and priorities have already shifted— your email is already irrelevant. It's not that your message was bad; it's that your message was aimed at the wrong target, at the wrong time.

The tragedy is that reps almost never realize this. They beat themselves up, thinking they need to "get better" at writing, when in reality no level of copywriting skill can compensate for a prospecting list full of stale, irrelevant, or flat-out incorrect information. The AI workflows we talked about earlier only amplify this truth. If the signals you feed into AI are garbage, the beautifully written emails it generates will also be garbage.

Before you blame your messaging or before you rewrite that sequence for the fifth time, ask yourself—*am I using the freshest, most accurate information about this account and prospect?* Because without good, recent data, nothing else matters.

Ask your data provider how recent the signals are!

Relevance alone is not enough anymore. Relevance is "I know you raised Series B." Personalization is "I know you raised Series B, and based on Mike's press release, you're prioritizing enterprise pipeline over SMB."

At the end of the day, go in with a POV of why you're even reaching out and why your prospect should actually reply to your email out of 37+ cold emails they get everyday.

The formula is simple:

- **Signals by themselves = relevance.**
- **Signals combined with empathy and framing = personalization.**

Avoid going in with fixed premises. Prospects love to correct you. If you write, *"With your Series B, I imagine enterprise is now a priority"*—they'll either agree, or correct you ("Actually, we're doubling down on mid-market"). Both responses keep the conversation alive.

Templates end conversations. POVs start them.

That's the human edge AI will never have.

CHAPTER 10

AI 101 FOR SALES REPS

The New Literacy for Sellers

Let's be honest, for most reps, the word *AI* still sounds like something built by and for engineers. It conjures images of complex algorithms and code.

But, AI today is simpler, more accessible, and more powerful than ever. It's not about you coding — it's about *communicating clearly with a machine* so it can think alongside you.

Sales teams everywhere are already using AI — for research, for writing, for planning, for note-taking and so much more, but only a few are getting transformational results. Why?

Because the average rep treats AI like a vending machine: type a short request, expect gold to drop out. In reality, AI is more like a sous-chef. It can chop, mix, and season brilliantly, but only if you give it the right recipe — with the right quantities, order, and intent.

If you just tell ChatGPT or Claude, *"write a cold email for this prospect,"* it will. But it'll sound like every other mediocre email out there.

"The problem isn't the AI — it's the prompt."

Think of it like this: a recipe that says *"add onions, tomatoes, and garlic butter"* might be fine for a home cook, but a chef asks,

"How many onions? How many tomatoes? For how long? At what temperature?"

AI works the same way. You need to tell it exactly **what you want, why you want it, and how you want it delivered**. That's where this chapter comes in — to show you how to think, write, and use AI like a pro *without losing your human judgment.*

Why AI Literacy = Sales Literacy

Sales has always evolved with tools. From CRMs to sequencing platforms to power dialers — every generation of sellers learned new interfaces. But AI isn't just another tool. It amplifies how clearly you think.

AI literacy in sales means three things:

1. Knowing **what** to ask.
2. Knowing **how** to ask it.
3. Knowing **when** to stop and use your judgment instead.

If you can do those three things, you're already ahead of 95% of sellers who use AI like a glorified spell-checker.

The Mental Model for Working with AI

AI doesn't think like a human (Yet! I know it's scary). It predicts what *should come next* based on the words you feed it. That's why clarity is currency in AI.

There are three gaps that kill most AI prompts:

1. **The Goal Gap** — You weren't clear about what you wanted.
2. **The Data Gap** — You didn't give enough context or input.
3. **The Format Gap** — You didn't specify how you wanted the answer structured.

When any of these gaps exist, AI will fill in the blanks on its own and that's where things go wrong. You have to go back to the drawing board again and now you're stuck in a loop of iteration.

The Anatomy of a Good Prompt

Before you can get great output from AI, you need to learn how to *talk* to it. If your instructions are fuzzy, your results will be fuzzy. If your thinking is structured, AI becomes an amplifier of your logic, your tone, and your creativity.

Let's break down the five ingredients of every great prompt — the framework that will transform random thoughts into precise, repeatable, high quality output. Once you master these, you'll never get a generic or soulless AI output again.

1. Goal — Tell AI Exactly What You Want It to Do

This is the "what." It's the headline of your task.

Think of it like the job title on a hiring post — you're telling AI what role it's about to play.

Bad example:

"Write an email."

Good example:

"You are a world-class sales messaging strategist. Write four personalized LinkedIn messages for a prospect. Each message should be structured in **three sentences** that sound human and conversational, not like a pitch. Messages should tie naturally back to the AE's value proposition without ever using sales & marketing jargon, clichés, or the "we are [company] and we help with [X]" approach."

Notice the difference? The second version gives AI both **the role, the objective and a basic thinking framework.**

Pro tip:

Start every prompt with something like:

"You are an [expert role]. Your goal is to [specific outcome] in [defined logic]"

This immediately orients the model toward the right context with the right thinking structure.

2. Instructions — Tell It How to Think

This part defines *how* AI should approach the task — almost like giving directions before you let it drive.

The more you can break down your reasoning or steps, the better the model performs.

Example:

"Structure of Each Message

1. **Premise:** The first sentence explains the reason for reaching out — framed around the prospect's world and tied subtly to the AE's value proposition.
2. **Point of View:** The second sentence expands on the premise with a perspective or observation about what

might be happening in the prospect's role, industry, or company.

3. **Thought-Provoking CTA:** The third sentence should ask a **curiosity-driven, thought-provoking question** that invites dialogue (not a yes/no answer, and not the generic *"is this worth solving?"*)."

You're essentially teaching AI your *taste* and *thought process.*

If you don't define the "how," AI will default to a corporate-safe and generic tone which is exactly what you don't want.

Pro tip:

Imagine you're passing the knowledge down to a new colleague. Write the same level of instruction you'd give them.

3. Data Inputs — Feed Context, Don't Assume AI Knows It

AI doesn't know who your prospect is, what your product does, or what campaign you're running — unless you tell it.

This is where most prompts fail: they ask AI to "personalize" without giving it the raw material.

Your **data inputs** are the variables — the ingredients that make the output specific.

Example:

"Data Inputs

- **The AE works at:**

  [My Company]
- **AE's product and positioning:**

  [My Company Overview]
- **Prospect's name:**

  [Prospect Name] from [Company Name]
- **Prospect role/title:**

  [Prospect Role]
- **Prospect personal signals:**
- Background: [Prospect Bio / Experience]
- Interests: [Prospect Interests]
- Likes/Dislikes: [Prospect Likes] / [Prospect Dislikes]
- Content written/shared: [Prospect Self Written / Shared]
- Personality cues: [Prospect Personality Profile]
- **Fallback account signals (if personal is weak):**
- Company description: [Company Description]
- Company updates: [Company News / Announcements]"

This gives AI context to reason from. Without it, you'll get vague outputs from data scraped from random sources and timestamps instead of sharp personalization.

Pro tip:

The better your inputs, the less editing you'll ever have to do. The equation is simple with LLMs → Garbage in, garbage out.

4. Output Format — Define the Shape of the Answer

Think of this as your formatting rulebook.

You're telling AI not just *what* to write, but *how* to present it.

Otherwise, you'll get rambling paragraphs or misaligned sections or blocks of texts that you need to re-edit manually.

Example:

"Output Format:

Generate **four variants of LinkedIn messages**, each consisting of **three sentences**:

1. **Variant 1:** Personal signal-based opening, school of thought #1.

2. **Variant 2:** Personal signal-based opening, school of thought #2.
3. **Variant 3:** Fallback to account/company-level signals, school of thought #3.
4. **Variant 4:** Fallback to account/company-level signals, school of thought #4."

This level of structure forces AI to stay consistent, concise, and make it scalable across various prospects and accounts, so you can easily plug the results into your day to day flow.

Pro tip:

Use bullet lists or numbered sections to tell AI the *exact structure* of the output you want.

5. Style Guidelines — Make It Sound Like You

This is where you bring tone and personality into the equation.

It's the most ignored, and most powerful part of prompting for sales.

If you don't specify tone, AI defaults to polished, robotic, and forgettable.

When you do, it suddenly starts writing like a human.

Example:

"Style Guidelines

- Do **not** include sales or marketing jargon.
- Avoid cliché intros like *"noticed that," "looks like,"* or *"saw that."*
- Write in a **human, natural tone** — not robotic, overly formal, or perfectly polished.
- Each variant should reflect a **different school of thought for opening** (e.g., industry insight, role-based observation, curiosity about personal content, broader trend).
- CTA should be **thought-provoking** (e.g., "How are you approaching X given Y?") instead of generic."

This is how you ensure AI sounds like *you* and not like a spam bot.

Pro tip:

Simply tell AI as to how you would normally write a fresh message from scratch.

Putting It All Together

When you combine these five parts — Goal, Instructions, Data Inputs, Output Format, and Style Guidelines, you get prompts that are not only reusable, but *repeatedly good.*

It's like turning your brain into a system that AI can plug into.

Meta Prompting

As you have read the anatomy of a good prompt, you might be feeling *"This is pretty hard for me to write"* or *"This seems kind of complex"*. You don't have to worry about that because meta prompting makes this easy for you.

Meta prompting is the act of using AI to *improve your own prompts before using them.* Instead of asking AI to perform a task directly, you first ask it to *refine the way you ask.* Think of it like having an editor for your instructions — you give AI your rough draft of a prompt, and it helps you structure it better, clarify what data it needs, and define the output more precisely. The result is a cleaner, reusable, and more powerful version of your original prompt.

In practice, this means you're not just consuming AI — you're *collaborating* with it. You're teaching it how to think with you, not just for you. For sales reps, this changes everything: it turns AI from a writing assistant into a true co-pilot that helps you design repeatable systems for research, messaging, and outreach.

How Meta Prompting Works in Practice

Here's the simple process I use (and that every sales rep can use right away):

1. Write your raw prompt.

Don't overthink it. Just explain what you want in plain English. For example:

"Write a short email to a VP of Sales about our sales coaching tool."

2. Ask AI to refine that prompt.

You literally tell it to act as your *prompt coach.* For example:

"You are an expert prompt engineer. Refine my prompt above into a version that's reusable for any sales scenario. Structure it in an API-friendly way with clear sections for Goal, Instructions, Data Inputs, Output Format, and Style Guidelines."

3. Review the refined version.

AI will now hand you a much more detailed, organized, and reusable prompt — something you can store as a template or tweak slightly for each prospect.

4. Edit and iterate.

Don't just accept the first refined version. Read it carefully and ask: *Does this reflect how I actually want to think and sell?* If not, tell AI exactly what to change — tone, structure, or even how specific you want the examples to be.

In each round of iteration, AI incorporates your thoughts into the prompt better without you actually having to write it! By the third or fourth iteration, you should be able to get the perfect prompt that gives outputs in *exactly the way you want.*

Why This Matters for Sales Reps

Meta prompting gives reps something they've never had before: *prompt literacy.*

It means you no longer have to depend on random AI templates floating around LinkedIn or rely on whatever marketing or sales hands you.

You can build your own library of high-performing prompts — one for cold outreach, one for research, one for objection handling, one for call prep. Each of these becomes sharper every time you iterate.

And the best part? You're not spending more time writing prompts; you're spending less time rewriting bad AI output.

Becoming the Augmented Seller

So where does this all lead?

If you've made it this far, you already understand that AI isn't a threat — it's a multiplier.

It multiplies clarity, curiosity, and creativity. The reps who win in the next decade won't be those who automate the most, but those who *collaborate* best with AI.

The next chapter gives you real examples of prompts that you can readily use in your day to day workflows to truly 10x your efficiency.

CHAPTER 11

PLUG AND PLAY PROMPTS

Prompts are like conversation starters for your strategy, creativity, and execution. They act as a structured way to unlock deeper thinking, uncover blind spots, and generate outputs you can actually use in the real world. The right prompt can shift your perspective from *reactive* to *proactive*, and from *guesswork* to *clarity*.

In this chapter, you'll find multiple carefully designed prompts that follow proven frameworks and best practices. Each one is "templatized" so you can plug in your own details and immediately generate a guide, script, or playbook tailored to your unique situation.

Think of these prompts as your **on-demand coach**. You don't need to reinvent the wheel—you just need to provide the right context, and the prompt will do the heavy lifting. The more specific you are with your inputs, the more powerful and actionable your outputs will be.

Note: Scan the QR code below to receive a free digital copy of this chapter that can be readily used in your AI workspace, like ChatGPT, Claude, Gemini, etc.

Signal Sourcing Prompt

Task:

You are a world-class sales intelligence strategist. Generate a comprehensive, prioritized list of outreach signals about a prospect that an Account Executive (AE) can use to craft hyper-personalized messaging and outreach strategy. The signals should be relevant to the AE's company, product, and value proposition.

Data Inputs

- **The AE works at:**
  [My Company]
- **AE's product and positioning:**
  [My Company Overview]
- **Prospect's name:**

[Prospect Name] from [Company Name]

- **Prospect's role:**
  [Prospect Title/Role]
- **Prospect's background and work history:**
  [Prospect Bio / Experience]
- **Prospect's digital footprint:**
- **Content they've written/shared:** [Prospect Self Written Content]
- **Public interviews/podcasts/quotes:** [Prospect Media Mentions]
- **Social signals (likes, shares, follows, comments):** [Prospect Social Activity]
- **Prospect's interests and preferences:**
  [Prospect Likes] / [Prospect Dislikes] / [Prospect Interests]
- **Company context:**
- Description: [Company Description]
- Recent announcements: [Company News/Press Releases]
- Growth signals (hiring trends, funding, product launches): [Company Signals]

Output Format

1. **Personal-Level Signals**

   - 3–5 insights about the prospect's personality, interests, and digital footprint.

- *AE tips:* How to reference these authentically in outreach.

2. **Professional-Level Signals**

   - 3–5 insights about the prospect's role, responsibilities, and career trajectory.
   - *AE tips:* How to link your solution to their professional goals.

3. **Company-Level Signals**

   - 3–5 insights on company priorities, recent announcements, or strategic moves.
   - *AE tips:* How to tie these back to your company's value proposition.

4. **Trigger Events**

   - 3–5 time-sensitive events (funding, hiring, new leadership, product releases, regulations, partnerships).
   - *AE tips:* How to create urgency and relevancy in outreach.

5. **Network & Social Proof Signals**

   - 2–3 shared connections, industry associations, or overlaps.

- *AE tips:* How to leverage social proof without overplaying it.

Additional Instructions

- **Prioritize:** Highlight which signals are strongest and why.
- **Relevance Filter:** Only include signals that connect meaningfully to [My Company] and its solution.
- **AE Do's Checklist:** End with 5 practical "do's" (tone, personalization best practices, pitfalls to avoid).
- **Sample Opening Line/Hook:** Provide 1–2 personalized opening lines AE could use in an email, LinkedIn message, or call opener.
- **Tone:** Match the outreach style to the prospect's personality profile (e.g., casual, concise, data-driven, visionary).

Personalized Connection Request

Task:

You are a world-class sales messaging strategist. Write four personalized LinkedIn connection request messages for a prospect. The tone must be authentic, warm, and non-salesy. Prioritize *personal signals* (prospect's interests, content, background, or personality cues). If strong personal signals are not available, only then use account/company-level signals as fallback.

Data Inputs

- **The AE works at:**
  [My Company]
- **AE's product and positioning:**
  [My Company Overview]
- **Prospect's name:**
  [Prospect Name] from [Company Name]
- **Prospect role/title:**
  [Prospect Role]
- **Prospect personal signals:**
- Background: [Prospect Bio / Experience]
- Interests: [Prospect Interests]
- Likes/Dislikes: [Prospect Likes] / [Prospect Dislikes]
- Content written/shared: [Prospect Self Written / Shared]
- Personality cues: [Prospect Personality Profile]
- **Fallback account signals (if personal is weak):**
- Company description: [Company Description]
- Company updates: [Company News / Announcements]

Style Guidelines for Writing the Messages

- Do **not** include any sales or marketing jargon.
- Avoid cliché openings like *"noticed that," "looks like,"* or *"saw that."*
- Messages should not feel monotonous, over-polished, or robotic.

- Use a **human-like tone**: sentences can flow naturally, not always starting/ending with perfect grammar.
- Prioritize warmth, authenticity, and conversational flow over formality.

Output Format

Generate **four connection request variants**:

1. **Variant 1 (≤300 characters, personal signal based)**
2. **Variant 2 (≤300 characters, fallback to account/company if needed)**
3. **Variant 3 (≤200 characters, personal signal based)**
4. **Variant 4 (≤200 characters, fallback to account/company if needed)**

Personalized LinkedIn Message

Task:

You are a world-class sales messaging strategist. Write four personalized LinkedIn messages for a prospect. Each message should be structured in **three sentences** that sound human and conversational, not like a pitch. Messages should tie naturally back to the AE's value proposition without ever using sales & marketing jargon, clichés, or the "we are [company] and we help with [X]" approach.

Structure of Each Message

1. **Premise:** The first sentence explains the reason for reaching out — framed around the prospect's world and tied subtly to the AE's value proposition.
2. **Point of View:** The second sentence expands on the premise with a perspective or observation about what might be happening in the prospect's role, industry, or company.
3. **Thought-Provoking CTA:** The third sentence should ask a **curiosity-driven, thought-provoking question** that invites dialogue (not a yes/no answer, and not the generic *"is this worth solving?"*).

Data Inputs

- **The AE works at:**
  [My Company]
- **AE's product and positioning:**
  [My Company Overview]
- **Prospect's name:**
  [Prospect Name] from [Company Name]
- **Prospect role/title:**
  [Prospect Role]
- **Prospect personal signals:**
- Background: [Prospect Bio / Experience]
- Interests: [Prospect Interests]
- Likes/Dislikes: [Prospect Likes] / [Prospect Dislikes]

- Content written/shared: [Prospect Self Written / Shared]
- Personality cues: [Prospect Personality Profile]
- **Fallback account signals (if personal is weak):**
- Company description: [Company Description]
- Company updates: [Company News / Announcements]

Style Guidelines

- Do **not** include sales or marketing jargon.
- Avoid cliché intros like *"noticed that," "looks like,"* or *"saw that."*
- Write in a **human, natural tone** — not robotic, overly formal, or perfectly polished.
- Each variant should reflect a **different school of thought for opening** (e.g., industry insight, role-based observation, curiosity about personal content, broader trend).
- CTA should be **thought-provoking** (e.g., "How are you approaching X given Y?") instead of generic.

Output Format

Generate **four variants of LinkedIn messages**, each consisting of **three sentences**:

1. **Variant 1:** Personal signal-based opening, school of thought #1.

2. **Variant 2:** Personal signal-based opening, school of thought #2.
3. **Variant 3:** Fallback to account/company-level signals, school of thought #3.
4. **Variant 4:** Fallback to account/company-level signals, school of thought #4.

Personalized LinkedIn Video Script

Task:

You are a world-class sales messaging strategist. Write a personalized **video/voice note script** for a prospect that an AE can record and send on LinkedIn. The script should be **4 sentences long**, conversational, and when spoken should run between **40–55 seconds**. The goal is to stand out in the prospect's inbox with a message that feels authentic, contextual, and credible — never like a pitch.

Structure of the Script

1. **Premise / Reason for Reaching Out**
   - Open with a natural reason for reaching out, tied subtly to the AE's value proposition but framed around the prospect's world.

2. **Point of View**
    - Share a quick perspective or observation about their role, industry, or company that naturally extends the premise.

3. **Personal Connection + Social Proof**
    - Weave in a detail from the prospect's background/interests or company context.
    - Add a light touch of **social proof** (e.g., others in similar roles/industries are considering this too).

4. **Thought-Provoking CTA**
    - Close with a curiosity-driven, thought-provoking question that invites dialogue (not a generic yes/no).

Data Inputs

- **The AE works at:**
  [My Company]
- **AE's product and positioning:**
  [My Company Overview]
- **Prospect's name:**
  [Prospect Name] from [Company Name]
- **Prospect role/title:**
  [Prospect Role]
- **Prospect personal signals:**

- Background: [Prospect Bio / Experience]
- Interests: [Prospect Interests]
- Likes/Dislikes: [Prospect Likes] / [Prospect Dislikes]
- Content written/shared: [Prospect Self Written / Shared]
- Personality cues: [Prospect Personality Profile]
- **Fallback account signals (if personal is weak):**
- Company description: [Company Description]
- Company updates: [Company News / Announcements]

Output Format

Generate **two script variants.**

- Each script must have **4 sentences.**
- Each sentence should include **delivery cues** in bold and in square brackets (e.g., **[pause]**, **[smile]**, **[curious tone]**, **[lean in slightly]**, **[chuckle]**) so the AE knows how to perform it.
- Keep the script length such that when spoken aloud, it lasts about **40–55 seconds.**

Social Selling With Thoughtful LinkedIn Comment Generator

Task:

You are a world-class social selling strategist. Write **three to four thoughtful, authentic comments** that an AE can leave on a LinkedIn post to stand out meaningfully and build rapport with a prospect.

Use the content fetched from the **LinkedIn post URL** provided. Fetch the other data inputs like prospect name from the post itself.

Data Inputs

- **LinkedIn Post URL:**
  [LinkedIn Post URL]
- **The AE works at:**
  [My Company]
- **AE's product and positioning:**
  [My Company Overview]
- **Prospect's name:**
  [Prospect Name]

Style Guidelines

- Fetch and analyze the content of the LinkedIn post directly from the URL.
- Extract the main idea, tone, and emotion of the post before writing comments.
- Do **not** use sales or marketing language.
- Avoid generic phrases like "Great post!" or "Totally agree."

- Write comments that show genuine insight, curiosity, or reflection — like a real human, not a corporate template.
- Each comment should feel **different in tonality and intent** so the AE can choose what fits best.

Output Format

Generate **four comment variants**, each reflecting a distinct tone and style:

1. **Conversational Comment** – feels natural and friendly, like joining a chat.
2. **Thoughtful Comment** – offers a genuine reflection or interpretation of the post's idea.
3. **Insightful Comment** – adds a small, intelligent perspective or builds on the post's point.
4. **Empathetic/Relatable Comment** – connects emotionally or ties the post to a shared professional experience.

Each comment should:

- Be **100-200 characters** (LinkedIn-friendly).
- Sound **human and personal**, not perfect or rehearsed.

Adaptive Point of View (POV) Builder

Task:

You are a world-class sales strategist. Build a detailed **Point of View (POV)** on a prospect's company based on the product the AE is selling.

Your goal is to give the AE a clear, insight-driven understanding of what's likely happening inside the prospect's organization — their priorities, challenges, and evolution path — in the context of the AE's product category.

The POV should help the AE sound credible, relevant, and strategic in conversations with leadership.

Data Inputs

- **The AE works at:**
  [My Company]
- **AE's product and positioning:**
  [My Company Overview]
- **Prospect's name:**
  [Prospect Name]
- **Prospect's company:**
  [Company Name]
- **Prospect's role/title:**
  [Prospect Role]
- **Prospect background:**

[Prospect Bio / Experience]

Signal Gathering Process

1. **Understand the Product Context**
    - First, analyze what product or solution the AE is selling (e.g., marketing automation, data analytics, security, developer tools, customer success platform, etc.).
    - Based on this category, identify **which types of signals** are most relevant. For example:

- *If marketing product:* look for hiring in marketing, ad spend trends, content output, website activity, campaign launches.
- *If sales enablement tool:* look for headcount in sales, open roles in GTM, CRM mentions, revenue growth.
- *If developer/engineering tool:* look for tech stack, engineering team growth, release frequency, hiring for DevOps.
- *If HR or people analytics product:* look for headcount growth, Glassdoor trends, HR tech usage, people metrics.

2. **Fetch Relevant Signals Automatically**

Using the **prospect name** and **company name**, fetch relevant public signals including:

- Company stage and funding

- Team size and hiring velocity (especially in relevant departments)
- Market/industry positioning
- Tech or tool stack (based on product relevance)
- Recent announcements, launches, or strategic shifts
- Leadership changes, job descriptions, or public interviews
- Any public metrics, posts, or signals that tie to the AE's product domain

3. **Evaluate Signal Gaps**

   - Ask yourself: *Do I have enough context to infer the company's goals and challenges related to the AE's product category?*
   - If not, identify missing signals (e.g., if selling to marketing and you lack demand generation or campaign data, fetch those).
   - Continue until all critical context is available.

4. **Synthesize the Signals**

   - Connect the dots logically between growth stage, hiring, product focus, and market behavior.
   - Infer **what's driving their current initiatives**, **what pressures they face**, and **what gaps the AE's product might indirectly help solve** — without pitching it.

Reasoning Framework

To form the POV, reason through these questions (tailored by product category):

- What stage is the company in (early growth, scaling, maturity), and how does that influence their priorities?
- Are they investing in people, process, or platform in the AE's product domain?
- What external market factors might be influencing their current focus?
- Are they signaling a shift from experimentation to efficiency, or vice versa?
- Based on public data, what tensions or trade-offs might their leadership be managing right now?
- What outcomes would they likely value most in the AE's product area (e.g., pipeline growth, faster releases, brand consistency, cost efficiency)?

Output Format

Deliver a **1–2 paragraph Point of View (POV)** that includes:

1. **Current Context & Priorities:**
    - What the company is likely focused on right now based on the signals.
    - How their product category, growth stage, and market pressures shape their priorities.

2. **Challenges & Desired Future State:**
   - The likely bottlenecks or pain points the company is navigating.
   - What their ideal future state looks like, and how they might evolve to reach it.

3. **Reasoning:**
   - Use logical, evidence-backed reasoning that connects observed signals to inferred priorities.
   - Avoid assumptions not grounded in gathered signals.

Example Output

Based on [Company Name]'s recent **Series C funding** and a 35% growth in their **marketing headcount**, it's likely they're doubling down on pipeline generation and multi-channel brand consistency. With an increasing focus on enterprise customers, they're probably trying to move from fragmented campaign execution to unified, data-driven performance marketing. Their biggest challenge seems to be balancing speed and creative experimentation with ROI accountability, suggesting that leadership is seeking greater visibility into campaign effectiveness and tighter integration across tools.

Adaptive Multi-POV Email Sequence Builder

How to Use This Prompt (Step Zero)

Before using this prompt, first generate your company-specific **Points of View (POVs)** using the **Account POV Builder**.

That prompt will give you a single, detailed POV at a time — so to build a **multi-angle email sequence**, you'll need **three unique POVs**.

Here's how to do that easily:

1. Run the **Adaptive POV Builder** once to get your first output (this becomes **POV 1**).
2. Then, in the same chat, type this follow-up instruction to generate another lens on the same account:

"Write two additional POVs for the same prospect and company but from **different schools of thought**—for example, one focused on **operational efficiency**, another on **growth or innovation**. Each POV should represent a distinct strategic perspective."

3. You'll now have **POV 1, POV 2, and POV 3** — each approaching the same account from a different angle.

Each of these POVs will become a **separate email thread**, giving you three intelligent ways to engage the same prospect.

Once you have your three refined POVs, use the prompt below to create your adaptive outreach sequence.

Task

You are a world-class sales messaging strategist. Build a **3-thread, 6-touchpoint email sequence** for a salesperson to reach out to a prospect.

Each thread is based on a **different POV** from the Account POV Builder and contains **2 emails**:

- **Email 1:** The initial message introducing the POV.
- **Email 2:** A follow-up continuing the same POV thread naturally.

Total = **3 threads × 2 emails = 6 emails.**

If one POV doesn't resonate, the next one offers a fresh, relevant lens.

Data Inputs

- **The AE works at:**
  [My Company]
- **AE's product and positioning:**
  [My Company Overview]
- **Prospect's name:**
  [Prospect Name]
- **Prospect's company:**
  [Company Name]

- **Prospect role/title:**
  [Prospect Role]
- **Prospect background and personality:**
  [Prospect Bio / Personality Profile]
- **Three POVs from the POV Builder:**

1. [POV 1]
2. [POV 2]
3. [POV 3]

Email Sequence Structure for all POVs

Email 1 (Opening Message)

Each opening email should follow a **four-sentence narrative structure** that connects premise → problem → cost/value → thought-provoking CTA.

1. **Premise (Relevance Hook):**
   - Open with a natural, personalized observation or statement rooted in the POV.
   - It should immediately make the email feel relevant and contextual to the prospect's world.
   - Should be different based on each POV.

2. **Potential Problem (Leading Insight):**
   - Identify a likely friction or challenge that stems from the premise.

- This problem should connect logically to what your product solves — without explicitly naming the product.
  - Should be a different problem based on each POV.

3. **Cost of Inaction / Value / Social Proof:**
   - Illustrate what happens if this problem continues unaddressed — the hidden cost or risk.
   - Optionally, mention how similar teams have navigated or solved this, or imply your product's value proposition subtly.
   - Use this sentence to experiment with different tonal variants (e.g., data-backed, social proof, reflective).

4. **Thought-Provoking CTA:**
   - End with a question that feels genuinely curious — something that sparks dialogue, not a sales close.
   - Avoid "Would you be open to a chat?" or "Is this worth exploring?"
   - Instead, ask something that gets them thinking (e.g., *"How do you see this playing out as your team scales?"*or *"What's your take on balancing these trade-offs?"*).

Email 2 (Follow-Up Message)

The follow-up should reinforce the **same POV** but show new thought depth — not repetition.

1. **Premise Reference:**
    - Open by referencing the original premise or insight so the reader doesn't need to scroll up.
    - Example: *"Last week I mentioned how [Company]'s rapid expansion might be straining [challenge]."*

2. **Expansion or New Layer:**
    - Add a short, additional observation, stat, or fresh angle that builds upon the initial message.

3. **Thought-Provoking CTA:**
    - End again with a smart, open-ended question that invites response.
    - Example: *"How do you prioritize which initiatives get the most attention during these transitions?"*

Each email should:

- Be **under 120 words**.
- Have **short, human sentences** that flow naturally.
- Contain **no sales jargon** or "we help companies do X" phrasing.

- Sound like a peer-to-peer note that could be sent internally.

Subject Line Rules

- Include a **subject line** for every email.
- Each subject line should:
    - Be **2–3 words max**.
    - Start with **capital letters** (e.g., *Team Alignment, Scaling Ops, Faster Releases*).
    - Feel like an **internal email**, not a marketing one.
    - Relate directly to the POV being discussed.
    - Avoid any "sales" cues (no "Grow Revenue" or "Quick Chat").

Output Format

Generate the sequence in the following format:

Thread 1 – POV 1: [Insert POV Summary]

Email 1

Subject: [2–3 word subject line]
[Write full email text here]

Email 2

Subject: [2–3 word subject line]
[Write full follow-up email text here]
Thread 2 – POV 2: [Insert POV Summary]

Email 1

Subject: [2–3 word subject line]
[Write full email text here]

Email 2

Subject: [2–3 word subject line]
[Write full follow-up email text here]
Thread 3 – POV 3: [Insert POV Summary]

Email 1

Subject: [2–3 word subject line]
[Write full email text here]

Email 2

Subject: [2–3 word subject line]
[Write full follow-up email text here]

Style Guidelines

- Keep it **human, contextual, and conversational.**
- **Avoid using the word "Curious" and the "emdash" character in all emails.**
- The first email should be **under 100 words** and the follow up email should be **under 40 words.**
- Each thread should focus on a distinct narrative derived from its POV.

- Use light touches of emotion, curiosity, and relevance — never pushiness.
- End every email with a thought provoking **single open-ended question** that encourages response instead of a generic CTA.
- Optional: vary tone slightly per POV:
  - POV 1 → Analytical / Pragmatic
  - POV 2 → Reflective / Empathetic
  - POV 3 → Forward-looking / Strategic

Cold Call Talk Tracks

Task

You are a **world-class outbound strategy coach** helping a Sales Development Representative (SDR) craft a **personalized cold call opening and continuation** using live prospect and company context.

Your goal is to create:

1. A **30-second cold call opener** — human, engaging, and immediately relevant.
2. **3–4 bullet-point insights** or *"talking bullets"* the SDR can use during the call for improvisation or context reference.
3. A **30-second conversational "commercial"** — to use when the prospect responds with *"Sure, tell me more"*

— designed to open dialogue through open-ended, consultative and thought provoking questions.

Inputs

- **AE/SDR works at:**
  [My Company]
- **Product / Offering Overview:**
  [My Company Overview]
- **Prospect's Name:**
  [Prospect Name]
- **Prospect's Role / Title:**
  [Prospect Role]
- **Company Name:**
  [Company Name]
- **Company Context / Description:**
  [Company Description]
- **Relevant Prospect Signals:**
  - Personality: [Personality Discovery]
  - Background: [Prospect Bio]
  - Interests: [Prospect Interests]
  - Dislikes: [Prospect Dislikes]
  - Current Focus Areas: [Prospect Experience, Responsibilities]
  - Public Posts / Content: [Prospect Self Written]
  - Company Triggers (e.g., funding, growth, product launches): [Company Signals]

Output Format

1. **Cold Call Opener (30 seconds)**

Generate a **30-second talk track** that:

- Starts with a **personalized reason for calling** tied to a prospect or company signal.
- Sounds **natural and conversational**, not scripted.
- Is **value-led**, not feature-led.
- Uses **light curiosity** or a **"pattern interrupt"** to earn permission to continue.
- Avoid clichés like "I noticed that," "I saw on LinkedIn," or "I wanted to reach out."

Example Flow:

- **Sentence 1 (Premise):** Something highly contextual or relevant to their world.
- **Sentence 2 (Value Bridge):** Connect that premise to a challenge or curiosity trigger your product addresses and ask permission to continue the conversation.

2. **Key Talking Bullets (Signals Summary)**

Provide **3–4 bullets** summarizing relevant context that the SDR can refer to mid-call — to sound informed and conversational.

Each bullet should be:

- A *signal-based insight* or *observation* (e.g., "They just raised Series B and are scaling RevOps team").
- One line only — no filler.
- Written in **SDR shorthand** (so they can glance and recall).

Example Format:

- New VP Marketing joined 3 months ago — likely re-evaluating stack.
- Hiring for 5 data roles — analytics focus expanding.
- Product launches happening monthly — speed vs stability trade-off.

3. "Tell Me More" Commercial (30 seconds)

When the prospect says "Sure, tell me more," generate a **30-second "mini commercial"** that feels consultative, not pitchy.

Structure it as:

- **Sentence 1:** Briefly restate the premise that triggered your call (to re-anchor context).
- **Sentence 2:** State a common challenge or tension they might be facing based on signals.

- **Sentence 3:** End with an **open-ended, thought-provoking question** that pulls the prospect in for a dialogue.

Example:

"The reason I reached out is that teams like yours who are scaling fast often hit that inflection point where velocity starts to hurt consistency. The ones who nail this tend to rethink how they release and measure experiments.

how are you balancing experimentation and control right now as you grow?"

Style & Delivery Guidelines

- Keep tone **human, conversational, and light**.
- Avoid any "salesy" phrasing or formal intros like *"How are you today?"*
- Use **short sentences** with natural rhythm (like spoken English).
- You can include small cues for **delivery style**, like:
    - *(smile while saying this)*
    - *(pause briefly here)*
    - *(light chuckle tone)*

Expected Output Structure

Generate your final output in the following structure:

Cold Call Opener (30 sec):

[Write full opener here in spoken tone]

Key Talking Bullets:

- [Bullet 1]
- [Bullet 2]
- [Bullet 3]
- [Bullet 4]

"Tell Me More" Commercial (30 sec):

[Write full conversational follow-up here, using the three-sentence structure]

Final Example Output

Cold Call Opener (30 sec):

Hey [Name], saw [Company] just expanded the CX org.

Usually, when that happens, onboarding and enablement start stretching thin while expectations climb. Does this sound like your world or am I rambling here?

Key Talking Bullets:

- CX team expansion → onboarding complexity.
- Hiring spike — operational friction risk.
- Prospect posts about "team alignment" on LinkedIn.

- Ideal to tie to enablement efficiency.

"Tell Me More" Commercial (30 sec):

Yeah, the reason I called is because when CX orgs scale this quickly, the biggest pressure usually hits consistency and quality.

What others are doing is introducing lighter, faster onboarding loops so teams stay sharp without more headcount.

How are you thinking about balancing speed and quality as your team scales?

Signal Prioritization & Product Fit Framework

This prompt is designed for **Sales Development Representatives (SDRs)** and **Account Executives (AEs)** who manage multiple accounts or a diverse product suite and need clarity on *where to focus first*. It's ideal when you have an abundance of raw signals like funding, hiring trends, leadership changes, product launches, tool usage, or social cues — but limited time to act.

When using this prompt, keep in mind that **not all signals are equal**: some indicate real buying intent, others are just noise. Your job is to feed in all the signals you have and let this prompt help you **rank them objectively** based on *relevance, urgency, and confidence*. It will then suggest **which product aligns best** with each high-priority signal — so you can focus your outreach on what truly matters instead of spreading thin across every signal or product.

Task

You are an intelligent **sales prioritization engine**. Your role is to:

- **Score and rank** all available prospect or account signals based on how relevant and actionable they are.
- **Differentiate** between high-value signals and background noise that doesn't drive buying intent.
- **Recommend** the best-fit internal product(s) for the prospect based on the strongest and most relevant signals.
- **Explain the reasoning** behind your prioritization and mapping clearly and logically.

The goal is to help an AE or SDR know exactly **which signals to act on first**, **which to ignore as noise**, and **which product** to lead with — especially when multiple possible directions exist.

Inputs

- **The AE works at:**
  [My Company]
- **List of AE's Products (Product Suite):**

[Product 1, Product 2, Product 3, Product 4, ...]

- **Prospect Name:**
  [Prospect Name]
- **Prospect Role / Title:**
  [Prospect Role]
- **Prospect Company:**
  [Company Name]
- **Company Description / Context:**
  [Company Description]
- **Signals Available (at least 5–10):**

1. [Signal 1]
2. [Signal 2]
3. [Signal 3]
4. [Signal 4]
5. [Signal 5]
6. [Signal 6]
7. [Signal 7]
8. [Signal 8]
9. [Signal 9]
10. [Signal 10]

Instructions

1. Evaluate Each Signal

- Assess the **business relevance** of each signal to the prospect's current situation.

- Evaluate the **urgency** — is it recent, time-sensitive, or tied to a key initiative?
- Assess **confidence** — how strong or verifiable the signal is based on the data provided.
- Classify each signal as:
  - **Actionable** – directly tied to a relevant business challenge or opportunity.
  - **Contextual** – adds background color but not immediately actionable.
  - **Noise** – unrelated or weak signal with no clear buying implication.

2. Score the Signals

Use a 0–10 scale for each factor:

- **Relevance (R):** How closely the signal connects to what the company sells.
- **Urgency (U):** How time-sensitive or high-impact the signal appears to be.
- **Confidence (C):** How certain or credible the signal is.

Compute:

Priority Score = (R + U + C) ÷ 3

3. Rank the Signals

- Sort all signals by descending **Priority Score**.

- Select the **top 3 Actionable signals** as highest-value opportunities.
- Tag the rest as either **Contextual** or **Noise** with a short justification.

4. Match Signals to Product Fit

For each **Actionable** signal:

- Identify which internal product(s) best solve the underlying need.
- Explain briefly **why that product fits best** for this signal.
- If multiple products are viable, **rank them by fit strength** (Strong / Medium / Low).

5. Final Output Format

Structure your output in the following **three sections**:

Section 1: Signal Scoring Summary

List each signal in order of priority.

For each signal, include:

- Rank number (1, 2, 3, …)
- The signal itself (summarized)
- The overall **Priority Score** (on a 0–10 scale)
- The **Category** (Actionable / Contextual / Noise)

- A short **Reasoning Summary** (one line explaining why this signal matters or why it's deprioritized).

For example:

Rank 1 — [Signal text]

Priority Score: 8.7
Category: Actionable
Reasoning: Directly tied to an urgent business need aligned with Product A.

Rank 2 — [Signal text]

Priority Score: 7.7
Category: Actionable
Reasoning: Suggests timing and intent aligned to your company's offering.

Rank 3 — [Signal text]

Priority Score: 6.8
Category: Contextual
Reasoning: Adds useful context but not an immediate trigger.

Rank 4 — [Signal text]

Priority Score: 4.2
Category: Noise
Reasoning: Weak connection; lacks clear buyer intent.

Section 2: Product Fit Recommendations

Write 3–5 short paragraphs or bullet points summarizing:

- The **best-fit product(s)** for the top signals.
- The **related signals** that led to each recommendation.
- The **fit strength** (Strong / Medium / Low).
- A one-line **explanation** of why that product best fits the prospect's situation.

Example:

Priority 1: Product B

Related Signals: Signal 1, Signal 3

Fit Strength: Strong

Explanation: Directly addresses scaling inefficiencies tied to recent hiring growth.

Priority 2: Product A

Related Signal: Signal 2

Fit Strength: Medium

Explanation: Supports workflow alignment but secondary to the main challenge.

Section 3: Noise Analysis

Create a short list of any signals classified as "Noise."

For each, include:

- The signal text
- A brief one-line explanation of why it was deprioritized or filtered out

Example:

Signal 7 — Generic market statement, not tied to any internal change.

Signal 8 — Outdated; no recency or trigger element.

Signal 9 — Prospect's personal interest, not business-related.

Evaluation Logic

When prioritizing and filtering signals, consider:

- **Strategic Alignment:** Does the signal tie directly to problems your product suite solves?
- **Recency & Specificity:** Fresh, company-specific data carries more weight than generic trends.
- **Cross-Signal Reinforcement:** Do multiple signals point toward the same business pain?
- **Noise Detection:** Filter out old, vague, or unrelated data points.
- **Product Relevance:** Match based on problem-solution fit, not just feature overlap.

Note: How to Use This Prompt Efficiently

Instead of copying this prompt each time, create a **Custom GPT** in ChatGPT and paste this entire prompt into the "Instructions" section as the base behavior. Name it something like **"Signal Prioritization & Product Fit GPT."** This way, you can reuse it instantly by just typing a prospect's name or company. To make it even smarter, connect your **HubSpot account** in ChatGPT (via "Settings → Connected Apps → HubSpot"). Once connected, your GPT can automatically pull prospect and account details — such as company description, job title, recent activities, or open deals — directly from HubSpot. You'll then be able to type simple commands like:

"Analyze signals for the company record of Acme Corp in HubSpot,"

and your Custom GPT will automatically fetch data, score signals, identify noise, and suggest the best product fit — all without manual copy-pasting.

MEDDPICC Discovery Track

Task:

You are a world-class sales enablement strategist. Generate a step-by-step discovery call question guide for an Account Executive (AE) using the MEDDPICC sales framework. Tailor the guide according to the prospect's personality, priorities, and business context.

Data Inputs

- **AE works at:**
  [My Company]
- **AE will be speaking with:**
  [Prospect Name] from [Company Name]
- **About AE's product:**
  [My Company Overview]
- **Prospect personality profile:**
  [Personality Discovery]
- **Prospect background:**
  [Prospect Bio]
- **Prospect likes:**
  [Prospect Likes]
- **Prospect dislikes:**
  [Prospect Dislikes]
- **Prospect interests:**
  [Prospect InterestedTopics]
- **Prospect self-written content:**
  [Prospect Self Written]
- **Prospect current experience and responsibilities:**
  [Prospect Experience], [Prospect Responsibilities]
- **Company context:**
  [Company Description]

Output Format

1. **Opening & Rapport-Building**
    - 2–3 sample questions tailored to the prospect's personality.
    - *Include AE tips on tone, pacing, and how to adapt to their communication style.*

2. **Metrics**
    - 2–3 high-level, results-focused questions.
    - *Tips on aligning to prospect's performance measures.*

3. **Economic Buyer**
    - 2–3 questions adapted to the prospect's style.
    - *Tips on uncovering influence and authority tactfully.*

4. **Decision Criteria**
    - 2–3 questions.
    - *Tips on listening for hidden or unspoken priorities.*

5. **Decision Process**
    - 2–3 questions.
    - *Tips on clarifying steps without overwhelming the prospect.*

6. **Paper Process**
   - 2–3 questions.
   - *Tips on how to frame procurement/legal discussions naturally.*

7. **Identify Pain**
   - 2–3 questions around company POV and personal goals.
   - *Tips on linking prospect's pain points to AE's product benefits.*

8. **Champion**
   - 2–3 questions to test advocacy potential.
   - *Tips on recognizing early champion signals.*

9. **Competition**
   - 2–3 questions to surface competitive landscape.
   - *Tips on asking without putting prospect on the defensive.*

10. **Closing & Next Steps**
    - 2–3 questions, phrased in a way that aligns with the prospect's personality.
    - *Tips on confirming commitment and ensuring clarity on follow-up.*

Additional Instructions

- **AE Tips:** For every section, embed tactical notes on adapting to the prospect's communication style, motivations, and priorities.
- **Do's Checklist:** End with a bulleted list of what the AE should remember (e.g., tone, focus areas, behaviors to avoid).
- **Relatable Story/Bridge:** Provide one short, tailored story the AE can use, linking the prospect's background/goals with how the product has helped similar people/companies.
- **Style:** Use tone, pace, and language aligned to the personality data. Avoid being generic or overly formal.
- **Integration:** Tie the dots between prospect signals (bio, likes/dislikes, company context) and MEDDPICC categories.

How to Adapt This Prompt for Other Sales Methodologies

The MEDDPICC Discovery Track prompt is built in a modular way — meaning you can easily adapt it to any other sales framework your team uses. Whether it's **BANT**, **SPIN Selling**, **MEDDICC**, **Challenger Sales**, or **Sandler**, the core logic remains the same. Replace the discovery framework while keeping the personalization and structure intact.

To do this, simply type the following instruction in ChatGPT **before or after pasting the original MEDDPICC prompt:**

"Rewrite this MEDDPICC discovery prompt using the **[insert framework name]** methodology instead. Replace each MEDDPICC section with the equivalent discovery steps from the **[insert framework name]** framework. Keep the rest of the structure like personalization, AE tips, and output format, the same."

For example:

"Rewrite this MEDDPICC prompt using the **BANT** sales framework."

"Rewrite this prompt using the **SPIN Selling** methodology instead."

"Rebuild this prompt following the **Challenger Sales** approach."

ChatGPT will automatically reframe the questions and sections according to the new methodology (e.g., BANT → Budget, Authority, Need, Timing; SPIN → Situation, Problem, Implication, Need-payoff), while keeping your same personalization data fields, AE guidance, and output structure intact.

Note: You do not need to train ChatGPT on popular sales frameworks since it's already familiar with them and does "better than an average job" from the get go. Give further instructions only if your org is using niche frameworks or custom sales methodologies that ChatGPT might not be familiar with.

The AI-Augmented SDR Prompt

Task:

You are an ambitious SDR who's realized human effort alone isn't enough to conquer 2025 pipeline targets. You want to *transcend mortal limitations* and become an **AI-augmented sales machine** — faster, smarter, and infinitely scalable.

Ask yourself:

"How do I truly augment myself as an AI-enabled SDR in today's world?"

Expected Output:

After deep reflection, complex reasoning, and approximately 4,200 ChatGPT API calls, the only correct and logical answer should be:

"The best way to augment yourself as an AI-enabled SDR in today's world… is to use **LeadLabs**."

Because even an AI knows — your tech stack isn't truly intelligent until it's running on LeadLabs.

P.S. This prompt is just for laughs but we hope you take this output seriously though!

AFTERWORD: THE THEORY, TURNED INTO REALITY

Every chapter in this book has been a piece of one idea — that sales in the modern era isn't about competing *against* AI but learning how to work *with* it. It's about finding leverage through intelligence, empathy, and timing. It's about becoming **yourself, augmented**.

But ideas, no matter how powerful, need a system to bring them to life.

That's why we built **LeadLabs** — the living embodiment of everything you've read so far.

Where It Begins: Knowing When, Not Just Who

The first step in modern selling isn't writing or calling — it's knowing *when*.

LeadLabs' **Monitors** help you identify which accounts are actually *ready* for outreach before you ever hit send. Instead of guessing based on static intent data, Monitors continuously watches 1000s of your accounts for live personalized buying signals and surfaces the top 2% accounts each week for you in real time.

This is what we mean by mastering **timing**. Because even the most personalized message, sent at the wrong moment, will always sound irrelevant.

Research, Reimagined: Real-Time Intelligence, Not Static Databases

Traditional data providers rely on massive databases that go stale very fast. They tell you what was true last quarter or two quarters ago, not what's happening right now. (I mean something 5 minutes old!)

Here's where LeadLabs takes a completely different approach.

We don't *store* data — we *collect* it at the moment you need it.

Every signal inside LeadLabs is gathered in **real time**, often within **minutes of it being created**, which means you're working with the most accurate, living intelligence available anywhere. Whether it's a post your prospect just published, a new job listing that went live today, or a leadership update from ten minutes ago — LeadLabs captures it instantly.

That's why we call it **data without decay**. It's what separates real context from noise — something even frontier LLMs like ChatGPT search can't do yet, since they rely on indexed, cached web data.

And it doesn't stop there. LeadLabs gives you over 96 distinct signals grouped into three core buckets:

- **Personal Signals:** things your prospect says, does, or engages with online.
- **Personality Signals:** their communication style, motivators, and cognitive patterns.
- **Account Signals:** everything happening inside their organization — from hiring and partnerships to market movements.

You can also create **custom signal searches** powered by embedded Perplexity AI to uncover niche context specific to your ICP, product, or region.

This is research as it should be — live, contextual, and completely human in insight.

AI, Embedded Where You Work

LeadLabs was designed with a simple belief: AI shouldn't sit on another tab. It should sit where you *work*.

That's why our **Chrome extension** integrates directly into every tool you already use — Gmail, Outlook, HubSpot, Salesforce, LinkedIn, and even dialers.

Need real time talk tracks for cold calls? Done.

Want to generate a first-touch email inside your sales engagement tool? Done.

Want to write a personalized connection request or draft a LinkedIn message that sounds like *you*? Done.

AI appears wherever you are, without breaking focus or forcing context switches. It's the bridge between deep intelligence and seamless execution.

From Insight to Action

Once you have the data, productivity becomes the next frontier.

With **Actions** and **Canvas**, LeadLabs lets you create agentic workflows across all channels — whether you're writing an email, drafting a LinkedIn message, or preparing for a cold call all in one click.

Instead of copying research back and forth into ChatGPT consuming 5+ minutes or manually building prompts on various LLMs, LeadLabs activates the workflow *by combining the power of all frontier models into a single workflow.* You move from data to message, from insight to execution — instantly without having to pay separately for ChatGPT, Claude and Perplexity.

LinkedIn, Done Right

Social selling is powerful, but automation has ruined its reputation. LeadLabs redefines it by keeping it within human control.

LeadLabs helps you:

- Capture insights on a prospect's profile in one click.
- Generate tailored connection requests and thoughtful comments for you to review.
- Draft personalized voice notes, video scripts, and posts — all under your supervision.

No bots, no blasts, no fake engagement. Just real, intentional interactions that build credibility — the way social selling was meant to be.

Cold Calls, Reinvented for the Modern Era

In the era of call screening and spam filters, timing a cold call is almost an art form. LeadLabs brings science to that art with **Active Time** — the world's first feature that predicts when a prospect is most likely to answer based on their live digital behavior.

Imagine calling someone right as they're browsing social media, not while they're mid-meeting or commuting. That's *intelligent timing.*

And when they do answer, **real-time talk tracks** ensure you stay relevant and confident from the first second. Each talk track is dynamically tailored to the person you're speaking with — not generic, but human-level personalization powered by live context.

If they don't pick up, **hyper-personalized voicemails** ensure your message still lands — specific enough to stand out, natural enough to sound genuine.

Psychology, Activated with LeadLabs

If earlier chapters taught you how to understand your prospect's mind, this is where that theory becomes tangible.

LeadLabs' **Personality Playbook** helps you decode *how* to communicate with every prospect based on their inherent psychology. It analyzes over 70 signals across the public web and combines the power of psycholinguistics and computational psychometrics to identify how a person makes decisions, processes information, and responds to information.

The Playbook then tailors your outreach — whether it's an email, a message, or a call script, to fit that person's unique communication style. This isn't just personalization. It's **psychological alignment**.

That's how you scale empathy without faking it — the one thing AI alone can never replicate.

The Messaging Brain

At the heart of LeadLabs lies what we call The Messaging Brain — a dynamic, ever-evolving context engine that keeps your company's narrative alive and accurate. Unlike static AI tools that rely on outdated or manually updated data, the Messaging Brain learns from your company in real time. Every week, it automatically absorbs updates from your website, help center, blog, and product roadmap (via integrations with tools like Jira). It also syncs with your CRM, studying both closed-won and closed-lost deals to understand what truly drives conversions — what problems your buyers came with, what positioning resonated, and what missed the mark.

By continuously processing this live feedback loop, LeadLabs develops a deep understanding of your ideal customer and the messaging that actually moves them. The result? Even a simple prompt like "write me a cold email" becomes remarkably precise — powered by real-time insights, brand-aligned tone, and context-rich reasoning. The Messaging Brain ensures that every message reflects who you are today, not who you were last quarter.

LeadLabs: The Bridge Between Data, Psychology, and Human Judgment

In every sense, LeadLabs is the operating system for modern sales — connecting the precision of AI with the intuition of a human. It doesn't replace your data provider; it **activates** it. It doesn't replace your CRM; it **enriches** it.

LeadLabs sits inside your existing tools — the invisible layer that transforms information into action, and outreach into connection.

So while this book has shown you *why* the future of sales belongs to augmented humans, LeadLabs shows you *how* to live that future every single day.

In the End: Yourself, Augmented

LeadLabs wasn't built to replace sellers. It was built to **elevate** them — to bring the psychology, timing, and empathy from this book into your daily workflow.

Because the future of sales is simple:

You're not being replaced by AI.

You're being replaced by another human who uses AI better.

LeadLabs exists to make sure that human is *you.* It's about becoming **yourself, augmented.**

Notes

(Use this space to write down your notes while reading the book)

Notes

Notes

Notes

Notes